KANJI IN MANGALAND

Volume 1

Basic kanji course through manga

Marc Bernabe
Veronica Calafell
Alberto Aldarabi

Illustrations:
Gea Cassinello

Translation:
Olinda Cordukes

Kanji in MangaLand Volume 1
Basic kanji course through manga.
By Marc Bernabe, Veronica Calafell and Alberto Aldarabi

Published by: *Japan Publications Trading Co., Ltd.,*
        1-2-1 Sarugaku-cho, Chiyoda-ku, Tokyo, 101-0064 Japan.

(First edition)
1st printing: July 2007
2nd printing: November 2013

Distributors
UNITED STATES:
   Kodansha USA, Inc. through Oxford University Press,
   198 Madison Avenue, New York, NY 10016.
CANADA:
   Fitzhenry & Whiteside Ltd., 195 Allstate Parkway, Markham,
   Ontario L3R 4T8.

ISBN: 978-4-88996-221-5

Printed in China

IN DEAR MEMORY OF CO-AUTHOR
AND DEAR FRIEND ALBERTO ALDARABI

MARC BERNABE (L'Ametlla del Valles, Barcelona, 1976) is a Japanese-Spanish / Catalan translator and interpreter, with special emphasis on manga and anime translations, in addition to specializing in Japanese language and culture didactics for Spanish speakers. Among his works are the five-book *Japanese in Mangaland collection* (Japan Publications), as well as other books on Japan for the spanish speaking world. http://www.nipoweb.com

VERONICA CALAFELL (Palau de Plegamans, Barcelona, 1978) is a Japanese translator and interpreter, specializing in translation of entertainment products. She has lived several years in Japan, where she combined her translation job with her specialization in International Relations.

ALBERTO ALDARABI (Toledo, 1973 - Madrid, 2009) used to work in manga and anime translation, after graduating in Japanese from the Official Language School of Madrid - Jesús Maestro. Besides being editor of the magazine *Shirase* between 2001 and 2003, he was linked to the whole *Japanese in Mangaland* series, as well as collaborating in various projects related to Japanese language and culture. He sadly left us in 2009.

GEA CASSINELLO (Almeria, 1981) is a graphic designer, illustrator, and artist. She has collaborated in several comic-book and manga magazines and fan magazines. Recently, she has alternated art exhibitions and projects for the Almeria Council with several design courses. Now settled in Barcelona, she takes part in the new *Kanji in Mangaland* series of books.

Table of contents 目次

Introduction はじめに

You are holding the first of a series of three books aimed at teaching you the first 1006 漢字 kanji in Japanese writing, the so-called 教育漢字 *Kyōiku kanji* (*kyōiku* means "education"). The *Kyōiku kanji* are called so because they are the kanji Japanese children learn systematically during their six years in Elementary School (from 6 to 12 years old) as part of their basic education. This list is established by the 文部科学省 Japanese Ministry of Education and Science.

The idea of creating a new method in a widely explored field like kanji arose on noticing two facts. First, the enthusiasm with which young students and lovers of the Japanese language received the *Japanese in MangaLand* method. The series is currently published in several languages and consists of three textbooks and three exercise books, through which students can reach an intermediate level in Japanese. This will qualify them to pass levels 3 and 4 of the 日本語能力試験 *Nihongo nōryoku shiken* (or 能験 *Nōken*), the official test for Japanese as a foreign language. *Japanese in MangaLand* came to fill in a gap in the educational material for studying Japanese as a foreign language: that of texts aimed at teenagers and young adults. Furthermore, in a time when Japanese pop culture is driving people wild wherever it goes —due to the influence and widespread distribution of products such as videogames, manga, cartoons, or cinema— young people are developing, more and more, an interest towards everything related to Japan; an interest which, in the linguistic arena, few have considered fulfilling before *Japanese in MangaLand*. These teenagers are becoming younger and younger, and here we find the second fact that drove us to creating *Kanji in MangaLand*. Those who become interested in Japan and the Japanese language do so at an increasingly younger age; therefore, their study tools must also be suitable for their age, as well as for their cognitive abilities and their process of assimilating ideas.

To date, we observe two Japanese kanji teaching methods for foreigners. The first is the traditional method, where the study of kanji is approached in a similar way to that used in Japanese schools —by following an arbitrary order, consisting of the repetition of writing characters over and over again, until the kanji (or the movement of the hand when writing it), is engraved in the pupil's memory. The second method was introduced by professor James W. Heisig (whom two of the authors of this present work have had the honor of collaborating with on several occasions) and was based on the student's imaginative memory (see *Remembering the Kanji* I and II). To these two methods we now add a third one: *Kanji in MangaLand*, a method based on visual memory. This method will enable young students to tackle the study of kanji even if their capacity for abstract conception is not as fully developed as it may be at an adult age; or, alternatively, without the need of making a mental effort as demanding as with other methods.

Kanji in MangaLand combines the best of the two methods described above. On the one hand, it introduces kanji, with some order variations, just as they would appear in Japanese schools. That is, first, the most basic and commonly used; and, afterwards, the most complex ones. Each kanji comes with its most frequent readings, a breakdown of its writing, alternative spellings, number of strokes, and a good number of compounds, which makes this a valuable reference book even for advanced students. On the other hand, each kanji is represented as a set of amusing pictures, all equally flamboyant (each sub-picture represents a forming element of the whole kanji), which make its identification and subsequent memorization much easier. This aspect of *Kanji in MangaLand* is clearly original and different from any other books on kanji that you may find on the market, making it the trademark of this book, along with the rest of the "MangaLand" series. Why get bored studying if there are more enjoyable ways, which are equally, if not more, effective and, besides, use the cool art of manga as a tool?

Kanji in MangaLand combines (as does its father, *Japanese in MangaLand*) the study of kanji with the motivation which drives many people to study it: the Japanese style of manga art. Our method allows you to study kanji not as isolated entities, but as real words in context because we provide you with an original short story of one manga page for each lesson you study.

Everybody can use *Kanji in MangaLand*. Those students who have already initiated themselves in the study of Japanese, either with a teacher or self-taught, will find this book to be a supplement to their study and a backup for kanji (probably the main difficulty a Westerner comes across when learning Japanese). In addition to reading some original manga pages, beginner-intermediate level sentences and texts are used, which will allow the student to practice their knowledge of grammar. Even if they don't know anything about the Japanese language, those curious about kanji will find in this book a system to help them remember, identify, and learn how to write the characters since all texts and sentences in the book have been translated. Our purpose of using kanji in context is that of creating a real framework to learn the language —understanding kanji is not an isolated entity, but one part of a system as a whole.

Kanji in MangaLand is obviously a member of the "MangaLand" family, and, as such, it is designed to complement the three textbooks and the three exercise books in the *Japanese in MangaLand* series. While the primary focus of the last three is on Japanese grammar and vocabulary, they never leave writing aside. However, for obvious space reasons, they push the aspect of writing into the background. Thus, the need arose to create these three *Kanji in MangaLand* volumes, in order to provide an equally fun and innovating method to study kanji. However, Japanese is not only kanji, nor is it only grammar. Therefore, we highly recommend that students work simultaneously with the textbooks *Japanese in MangaLand* 1, 2, 3, and their corresponding exercise books, to consolidate the study of grammar and vocabulary; and the *Kanji in MangaLand* volume that is appropriate to their level.

This method will consist of three books, each containing two of the six grades in which the 教育漢字 *Kyōiku kanji* are divided. The books are structured in lessons of 8 or 12 kanji, to which we add one page of a manga-comic, one page of exercises, answers to the exercises, and a translation of the comic-book. We must state that *Kanji in Manga-Land* is a progressive study method, which means that what has been learned in a lesson is considered as assimilated in successive lessons and, therefore, what has been learned in the first book will be applied in the second and third books. Thus, we do not recommend that you start studying with this method from book 2 or 3.

Japanese writing

Japanese writing is the result of a combination of three writing systems:

KANJI: The subject of study in this book. They are complex characters "imported" from China to Japan in the 6th century, which represent "ideas" or "concepts" (that is why they are also called "ideograms").

HIRAGANA: One of the two syllabic alphabets or "syllabaries," with cursive forms.

KATAKANA: The second of the Japanese syllabaries, with rectilinear forms.

We only have documentary evidence of written Japanese from the 5th and 6th centuries and on; before this, Japanese language was oral, and had no writing system. In this period, Chinese ideograms (or kanji) were introduced into Japan, and were originally only used phonetically, but soon went on to be used ideographically to represent Japanese words. These kanji were imported along with their readings. Although, due to the need to adapt them to a preexistent language (oral Japanese), they were also given new readings. The result is this: one kanji can have several readings, which derive from their 音読み *on'yomi* (Chinese reading) and 訓読み *kun'yomi* (Japanese reading). This fact really complicates the Japanese writing system, even in comparison to the Chinese, where readings are for the most part univocal.

Nowadays, there are 1,945 "common use" kanji (常用 *Jōyō kanji*) of compulsory learning in elementary and high school, which enable you to read, with no trouble, all kind of texts in common Japanese. Among these, only 1,006 (the 教育 *Kyōiku kanji* in *Kanji in MangaLand*) are systematically taught during the six years at elementary school. The rest are gradually learned as years of study and reading draw on. An average Japanese person usually recognizes about 3,000 kanji; it is worth mentioning that among them are the 人名漢字 *Jinmei kanji* (kanji for people's names), which consist of almost 600 characters mainly used in first names and recognized by almost everybody.

The kana

Hiragana and katakana are a series of characters which represent a sound consisting of a simple vowel or formed by a consonant plus a vowel. Together, they are generically called 仮名 *kana* (syllabic alphabets of the Japanese language).

Since there was no native writing system in Japan with which the Chinese kanji could merge, and because Chinese and Japanese sounds are substantially different, during several centuries about 970 Chinese characters were used as phonetic symbols for the 88 Japanese syllables, giving birth to an older katakana syllabary. Halfway through the 8th century, some of these kanji were transformed into more cursive, curved lines, mainly by women in court during the Heian period (794-1185). They became the origin of the development of a phonetic syllabary with a univocal relationship between sound and written form. In the 10th century, this syllabary was recognized as an official writing system: hiragana. Nowadays, hiragana is used to write characteristic Japanese words, to add grammatical desinences, and to write those words with difficult or non-standard kanji.

Katakana forms also derive from kanji, but unlike hiragana they were not based on the calligraphic writing. Instead, a "part" *(kata)* of a kanji was taken to represent sounds. These forms were written in a rectilinear style. Nowadays, katakana is used to write foreign language loanwords (including proper nouns), to draw the reader's attention to a specific word, and for onomatopoeia.

In *Kanji in MangaLand,* because the kana are used to indicate kanji readings, knowledge of the kana syllabaries is essential. Thus, following the traditional convention, the 訓読み *kun'yomi* reading of a kanji will be indicated in hiragana, while the 音読み *on'yomi* reading will be in katakana. If you already have some experience in the study of Japanese, you should already know the kana (hiragana and katakana) syllabaries, and be able to read and write them; if so, then you can skip the next part and jump to the section entitled "How to use *Kanji in MangaLand.*" But if such is not your case, then keep reading and use this section to learn the kana; thus, overcoming the first obstacle in the Japanese language.

Hiragana table

あ a	か ka	さ sa	た ta	な na	は ha	ま ma	や ya	ら ra	わ wa	ん n
い i	き ki	し shi	ち chi	に ni	ひ hi	み mi		り ri	ゐ wi	
う u	く ku	す su	つ tsu	ぬ nu	ふ fu	む mu	ゆ yu	る ru		
え e	け ke	せ se	て te	ね ne	へ he	め me		れ re	ゑ we	
お o	こ ko	そ so	と to	の no	ほ ho	も mo	よ yo	ろ ro	を wo	

Katakana table

ア a	カ ka	サ sa	タ ta	ナ na	ハ ha	マ ma	ヤ ya	ラ ra	ワ wa	ン n
イ i	キ ki	シ shi	チ chi	ニ ni	ヒ hi	ミ mi		リ ri	ヰ wi	
ウ u	ク ku	ス su	ツ tsu	ヌ nu	フ fu	ム mu	ユ yu	ル ru		
エ e	ケ ke	セ se	テ te	ネ ne	ヘ he	メ me		レ re	ヱ we	
オ o	コ ko	ソ so	ト to	ノ no	ホ ho	モ mo	ヨ yo	ロ ro	ヲ wo	

VELARIZATIONS: adding two tiny strokes on the top right part of some kana, we obtain the so-called "impure sounds": voiced (or velarized) versions of these kana. This phenomenon affects "k," "s," "t," and "h" columns:

Hiragana: が (ga); ぎ (gi); ぐ (gu); げ (ge); ご (go); ざ (za); じ (ji); ず (zu); ぜ (ze); ぞ (zo); だ (da); ぢ (ji); づ (zu); で (de); ど (do); ば (ba); び (bi); ぶ (bu); べ (be); ぼ (bo).

Katakana: ガ (ga); ギ (gi); グ (gu); ゲ (ge); ゴ (go); ザ (za); ジ (ji); ズ (zu); ゼ (ze); ゾ (zo); ダ (da); ヂ (ji); ヅ (zu); デ (de); ド (do); バ (ba); ビ (bi); ブ (bu); ベ (be); ボ (bo).

On the other hand, adding a small circle on the top right part of the kana in the "h" column, we obtain the occlusive versions of these kana:

Hiragana: ぱ (pa); ぴ (pi); ぷ (pu); ぺ (pe); ぽ (po).

Katakana: パ (pa); ピ (pi); プ (pu); ペ (pe); ポ (po).

DIPHTHONGS: another essential point in order to use kana perfectly is knowing about diphthongs, which are combinations of the characters in the "i" line with those in the "y" line (the latter written in a smaller size):

Hiragana: きゃ (kya); きゅ (kyu); きょ (kyo); ぎゃ (gya); ぎゅ (gyu); ぎょ (gyo); しゃ (sha); しゅ (shu); しょ (sho); じゃ (ja); じゅ (ju); じょ (jo); ちゃ (cha); ちゅ (chu); ちょ (cho); にゃ (nya); にゅ (nyu); にょ (nyo); ひゃ (hya); ひゅ (hyu); ひょ (hyo); びゃ (bya); びゅ (byu); びょ (byo); ぴゃ (pya); ぴゅ (pyu); ぴょ (pyo); みゃ (mya); みゅ (myu); みょ (myo); りゃ (rya); りゅ (ryu); りょ (ryo).

Katakana: キャ (kya); キュ (kyu); キョ (kyo); ギャ (gya); ギュ (gyu); ギョ (gyo); シャ (sha); シュ (shu); ショ (sho); ジャ (ja); ジュ (ju); ジョ (jo); チャ (cha); チュ (chu); チョ (cho); ニャ (nya); ニュ (nyu); ニョ (nyo); ヒャ (hya); ヒュ (hyu); ヒョ (hyo); ビャ (bya); ビュ (byu); ビョ (byo); ピャ (pya); ピュ (pyu); ピョ (pyo); ミャ (mya); ミュ (myu); ミョ (myo); リャ (rya); リュ (ryu); リョ (ryo).

VOWEL LENGTHENING AND DOUBLE SOUNDS: the kana ended in "o" or "u" can have this last sound lengthened (that is, pronounced for a longer time than usual). This effect is indicated in hiragana adding the character う at the end. Thus, the diphthong しょう will be pronounced *shōh* (and not *shoU*, as could be thought), じゅう will be *juu*, びょう will be *byoo*, etc. When romanizing Japanese, this effect is usually represented with a dash on top of the lengthened "o" or "u;" thus, *ū* and *byō*. In this book, we will use the same method to indicate the lengthening in katakana: ジョウ (*jō*), ニュウ (*nyū*), ギョウ (*gyō*).

For phonetic reasons, and to make pronunciation easier, we sometimes have, as well, the phenomenon of "double sounds" (when the tongue sort of suddenly stops when pronouncing the sound). This effect is indicated with a small character っ (in hiragana) or ッ (in katakana) before the consonant to be doubled. This phenomenon only happens before those kana starting with *k, s, t, ch, g, z, d, b,* and *p.* Examples: まって (pronounced *matte*), バッド (*baddo*), あっし (*asshi*).

"WE" & "WI": you have probably noticed that in the "w" columns of the hiragana and katakana tables two forms corresponding to the sounds "we" (ゑ and ヱ) and "wi" (ゐ and ヰ) appear in grey. They are old forms whose usage was ceased after the language reform that took place at the end of the Second World War. You don't need to remember them, since in modern Japanese you will never come across them; they are included in the table for the sake of curiosity.

TO CONCLUDE: the explanations on kana we offer here are very basic and just enough for you to use this book without any other kind of help. However, we highly recommend that —in order to know more about their usage, pronunciation, and other characteristics— you resort to other more specific texts, such as *Remembering the Kana*, or *Japanese in MangaLand 1* and its exercise book.

At the end of this introduction you will find a table with the breakdown of the writing order for each syllabary: both hiragana and katakana.

How to use *Kanji in MangaLand*

Kanji in MangaLand is a self-learning method for kanji, designed for self-taught students, both for those who study Japanese grammar and vocabulary, and for those who don't. (Although, as we have mentioned before, we recommend the simultaneous study of the grammar and the writing, since knowing kanji alone is not very useful knowledge). Therefore, this book has all the necessary tools to be self-sufficient: readings for those kanji which have not yet been studied in the book; translations of the sentences in the exercises, of the manga pages, and of the review texts; and answers to all the drills we propose.

This book covers the first two grades of kanji studied at a Japanese school, which would be the equivalent to the program of the first two years at an elementary school. Lessons 1 to 7 cover the first grade (80 kanji), and lessons 8 to 21 cover the second (160 kanji). Altogether, providing you with a a course of 240 kanji for this first volume, which consists of two steps that you must climb in the suggested order. Book 2 will cover grades 3 (200 kanji) and 4 (200 kanji), while Book 3 (the final book) will cover grades 5 (185 kanji) and 6 (181 kanji). Altogether, we will study the 1006 *Kyōiku kanji*.

Even though we have chosen to follow the system of arranging kanji by grades as is done in Japanese elementary schools, we have opted to stray from the traditional order in which they are introduced because we find it to be unideal for students of Japanese. The Japanese school system generally introduces kanji of progressive complexity; that is, it usually introduces the simpler and most commonly used kanji in the first grades while leaving other peculiar, more technical kanji for higher grades —we find this is to be a very good idea. However, they sometimes tend to introduce complex kanji (such as 校) in their first grade, and much simpler kanji (such as 父) in their second grade. Because 父 is one of the radicals (that is, an element) of 校, ideally it should be introduced before 父. In spite of its faults, the arrangement into 6 grades is the most traditional and well-known; therefore, many students are familiar with it. Keeping this in mind, *Kanji in MangaLand* proposes an original arrangement, which will help the non-Japanese student who is unfamiliar with the kanji writing system. The arrangement that we have implemented is designed to help you remember and distinguish the characters, and tries to cover the criteria specified below:

DIFFICULTY: our course will first introduce the simpler kanji and then progress, little by little, in stroke number and complexity.

COINCIDENCE OR SIMILARITY OF ELEMENTS: the *Kanji in MangaLand* method is based on the pictorial representation of the "elements", or "radicals," which form each kanji. Sometimes, the element is a kanji in itself (as in 一, #1), as well as being an "element" in other kanji (本, #60, for example); sometimes, it's only an element in other kanji (as the *pregnant woman's belly* in 九, #25, and in 丸, #92). Sometimes, the elements are slightly deformed when forming part of another kanji (as happens with 火, #54, which sometimes becomes 灬). And, sometimes, some simple elements are combined to form a compound element to which we associate a new meaning (as the ヨ *trident*, the 冖 *tutu*, and the 巾 *apron*, which are combined to form the element for 帚 *housewife*, lesson 15).

DIFFERENTIATION OF VERY SIMILAR KANJI: in one same grade we will study the following kanji together: 大 *big*, #47, and 犬 *dog*, #48; 馬 *horse*, #230, and 鳥 *bird*, #231, so as to emphasize their differences and to avoid mixing them up.

SEMANTIC FIELDS, SYNONYMY, AND ANTONYMY: we group and learn the following kanji together: 父 *father*, # 212, 母 *mother*, #214, and 兄 *elder brother*, #215; those with very similar meaning, such as 戸 *door*, #131, and 門 *gate*, #132; or opposites, like 行 *go*, #136 and 来 *come*, #135.

The lessons

The lessons in *Kanji in MangaLand* consist of various parts. The first is the longest and is made up of the KANJI TABLES (we will explain in detail in the following section). These are in fact the essence of the book. All the necessary information related to the kanji studied in each case is included here. Most importantly, a picture representing the kanji is also given to remind us of its form. This helps express the image of an abstract entity as something concrete, something we can visualize, and later on reproduce when needed.

Besides different kinds of information, the kanji tables also offer a word list where the studied kanji is used in words called 熟語 *jukugo* (compound words). These are the words we will later find used in context in the following page: the MANGA page. This book contains 21 cartoon stories with which you can stop studying for a moment, have a pleasant break, and see in context, as well, the compound words and kanji you have studied. Those who already know grammar, can test their reading comprehension capacity with these manga stories; those who don't, can resort to the translation of the story (on the last page of each lesson). Thus, they can also follow the story, and still see the words they have learned in the real context of a Japanese text.

After the manga, a page of EXERCISES will help you practice your acquired knowledge. You can check whether you have memorized the kanji form with the pictures in the tables; whether you remember how to draw them in their correct stroke order; and how to read them depending on whether they are combined with other kanji or they are on their own, and depending on the meaning of the sentence. We have tried to find a balance between the reading and the writing exercises, as well as the mistake identification exercises, which are always helpful to prevent mistakes one could make later on.

Finally, in the last page of each lesson, we offer you the ANSWERS to the exercises, so that you can assess your progress; the TRANSLATION of the manga; and a look ahead at the NEXT ELEMENTS, which will be covered in the following lesson. The answers to the exercises are an essential component part of any self-taught learning method; remember you must use them for your assessment once you have finished the exercises, and not before.

At the end of the first grade, which covers lessons 1 to 7, we suggest you take a break: you have studied the equivalent of a full year course! Therefore, stop on the way, and complete the LEVEL 1 REVIEW, with which you can make sure that you have assimilated the knowledge acquired in the first seven lessons. Also, because your learning is cumulative, it is best to check that by the end of lesson 7 you still clearly remember what you studied in lesson 1. This is always true for the study of any language; but more so with kanji, since they are studied by "elements" which form each other. It is, after all, like building in your mind a gigantic Lego model. The same is to be applied to the LEVEL 2 REVIEW, at the end of the 21 lessons, which then prepares you for the second book.

To conclude, at the end of the book you will find two INDEXES. The first one is a kanji index, following the numerical arrangement of the kanji in the book, from 1 to 240; the second one is an index of readings in *rōmaji* (Roman letters), in alphabetical order. It is a joint index for both the readings of *on'yomi* and *kun'yomi*; the *on'yomi* in capital letters and katakana, and the *kun'yomi* in lower case letters and hiragana, which is the conventional and generally preferred method. With this index, you will be able to find any kanji, even if you only remember one of its readings.

The tables

The essence of *Kanji in MangaLand* is the kanji tables for study and their pictograms, which graphically represent each kanji. They are what make this learning method original and fun, besides making it suitable for a very wide age range. Here we have a kanji learning table, where we can see what its twelve parts have to show us:

Breakdown of a table

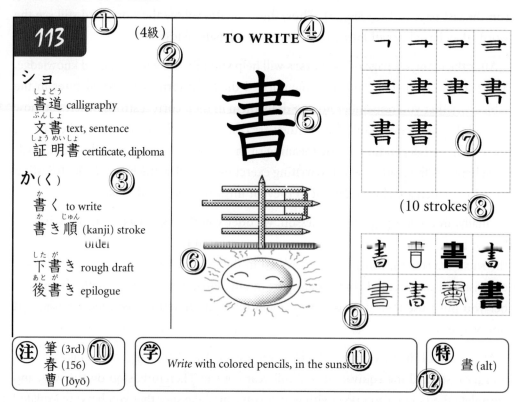

① **KANJI NUMBER**: its number in our method. Kanji will be numbered from 1 to 1006; this book will cover kanji numbers 1 to 240.

② **JLPT LEVEL**: level of the kanji in the official Japanese-language proficiency test. The JLPT standards differ quite a lot from the Ministry of Education, which is why we will surprisingly come across simple kanji which appear in advanced levels of the test (level 4 being the most basic, and level 1 the most advanced).

Note: This test was changed in 2010 and has now five levels (N1 to N5). However, the organizers have yet to publish any thorough list of the kanji for each level. This is why we will stick with the old system; just have in mind that N1 is roughly the equivalent of old level 1, level 2 has been divided roughly into N2 and N3, N4 is very similar to the old level 3 and N5 would be, more or less, equivalent to the former level 4.

③ **READINGS AND JUKUGO**: the reading or readings of the kanji we are studying (in katakana the *on'yomi* [Chinese reading], and in hiragana the *kun'yomi* [Japanese reading]), as well as several examples of *jukugo* (compound words). Be careful with velarization, occlusion, and sound division phenomenons (page 10) that some readings undergo in combination with other kanji to make their pronunciation easier, a perfectly normal occurrence. Unfortunately, in these cases, the only solution is to learn them by heart.

Examples:

In table 112, the *jukugo* 大声 is not read *ookoe*, but *oogoe* (velarization).

In table 88, 散歩 is not read *sanho*, but *sanpo* (occlusion).

In table 78, 学校 is not read *gakukō*, but *gakkō* (sound division).

In table 1, 一本 is not read *ichihon*, but *ippon* (sound division + occlusion).

④ MEANING: general meaning of the kanji.

⑤ KANJI: the kanji we are studying.

⑥ PICTOGRAM: picture representation of the kanji. Each "element," or radical, forming the kanji has been assigned a picture, and the sum of the various pictograms provides us with an effective and original way to remember the kanji. The slogan is: the more absurd and flamboyant, the better!

⑦ STROKE ORDER: detailed, step by step, order of strokes in which the kanji is written, which is very important in order to write it properly. There are certain rules, as well, for stroke writing order. Here we give the most basic ones. You should learn them by heart:

a) Kanji are written from top to bottom (see kanji #5 and #70 for clear reference).
b) Kanji are written from left to write (see #9, #106, and #139).
c) Horizontal strokes come before vertical strokes (see #31, #47, and #116).
d) The center portion comes before the strokes which flank it (see #49, #53, and #144).
e) The outside encasing comes before the inside (see #33, #34, and #182).
f) Strokes which bend toward the left come before strokes which bend toward the right (see #17, #57, and #212).
g) The stroke dividing the kanji from top to bottom comes after rules a-f (see #18 and #13).
h) The stroke dividing the kanji from left to right comes after rules a-g (see #76 and #77).

⑧ STROKE NUMBER: the number of strokes the kanji has.

⑨ OTHER KINDS OF WRITING: Japanese, like Western languages, evolved over hundreds of years. As a result, it has many styles of calligraphy with which it has been, and can be, written. Here we give different ways that you might find the same kanji (for example, in italics, bold, hand-written, artistic, primitive versions, historical versions, etc.). This list is only for your reference, and to help you identify kanji that you know, but which is written in a different style. Although we show you these variations, you should commit yourself to writing the kanji with the modern stroke order that we have provided.

⑩ EASILY CONFUSED KANJI: different kanji which can easily be confused with the kanji we are studying, usually due to similarity. The number after each kanji indicates its order in this book. "3rd," "4th," "5th," or "6th" indicates which of the corresponding grades of *Kyōiku kanji* that they belong to. Thus, the 3rd and 4th grades will appear in *Kanji in MangaLand 2*, while the 5th and 6th grades will appear in *Kanji in MangaLand 3*. When we indicate " Jōyō," it means the kanji is one of the 1130 "common use kanji"

(常用漢字 *Jōyō kanji*), which are not studied in elementary school. "not *Jōyō*" indicates the kanji is not in the list of *Jōyō* kanji.

⑪ **MNEMONIC CAPTION FOR THE PICTURE:** so that you can remember the picture better, and the kanji by extension, we offer a simple sentence using the elements and the general meaning of the kanji.

⑫ **ALTERNATIVE FORMS:** alternative or archaic forms of the kanji we are studying. We offer them basically for the purpose of reference, and you don't need to study them. "alt" indicates it is an alternative version; "old" an archaic form, now obsolete; "hom" indicates kanji which are read the same way and have similar meanings, though slightly different nuances of usage; and, last of all, "simp" indicates a simplified form of the kanji (generally used with handwritten kanji).

ふ
ほ

ね に う に
ー の ひ へ し
み む め も ゆ よ ら り
ー ヽ し っ い ー 、 ー
る ー ろ ー ー ん
を
わ そ

ね の は ひ ふ へ ほ ま み む め も や ゆ よ ら り る れ ろ わ を ん

は ふ む も や
に む も や
おかきけさせたちにぬ
ー い ー く い こ し ー そ ー ー つ て ー い

あ
き
た
な

おかきけさせ
かにこさすナちとナにぬ

あいうえおかきくけこさしすせそたちつてとなにぬ

アイウエオカキクケコサシスセソタチツテトナニヌ

ネノハヒフヘホマミムメモヤユヨラリルレロワヲン

Grade 1
小学校一年生

Lesson 1
第一課

New elements 新しい部首			
一 slice of bread		亠 Mexican hat	
十 faucet		八 spider legs	
三 sandwich		七 gymnast	
五 broken hourglass			

1 (4級)

ONE

イチ
いち
一 one (the number)
いちばん
一番 the first, the best
いちがつ
一月 January
いっかい
一回 once
いっぽん
一本 one (slender,
　　　 long thing), *ippon*

ひと(つ)
ひと
一つ one (item)
ひとり
一人 one person

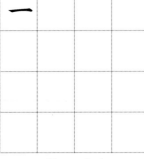

(1 stroke)

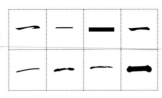

注

学 *One* slice of bread.

特 弐 (alt)
　 壱 (hom)
　 壹 (hom)

20

---

2 (4級)

**UP, TO RISE,
TO CLIMB**

ジョウ
いじょう
以上 more than
おくじょう
屋上 rooftop

うえ
うえ
上 above, up

あ(がる/げる)
あ
上がる to rise, to raise

のぼ(る)
のぼ
上る to climb (steps)
のぼ　　ざか
上り坂 upward slope

(3 strokes)

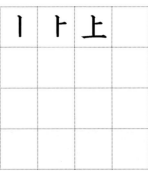

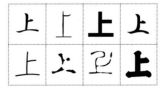

注 土 (55)
　 士 (4th)

学 We put jam on the bread with the faucet *on top*...

特 ⊥ (alt)

3

UNDER, TO GO DOWN, TO DESCEND

(4級)

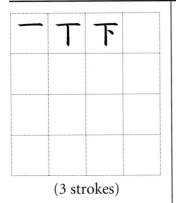

一 丁 下

(3 strokes)

カ / ゲ

地下鉄 (ち か てつ) subway (train)

下水 (げ すい) sewage

下痢 (げ り) diarrhea

した

下 (した) under

さ(がる)

下がる (さ) to descend

くだ(る)

下る (くだ) to go down

 特　丁 (alt)

学　...Because, if we put it with the faucet *underneath*, you won't have any jam.

 注　不 (4th)　干 (6th)

4

TWO

(4級)

一 二

(2 strokes)

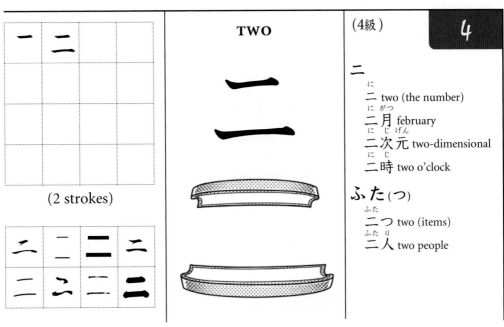

二

二 (に) two (the number)

二月 (に がつ) february

二次元 (に じ げん) two-dimensional

二時 (に じ) two o'clock

ふた(つ)

二つ (ふた) two (items)

二人 (ふた り) two people

 特　弍 (hom)

学　*Two* slices are better than one.

 注　三 (5)　乙 (Jōyō)

5 (4級)

THREE

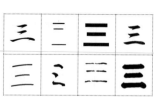

サン
- さん 三 three (the number)
- さんかい 三回 three times
- さんがつ 三月 March
- さんじゅう 三十 thirty
- さんかく 三角 triangle

みっ(つ)
- みっ 三つ three (items)
- みっか 三日 the third (day)
- み ご 三つ子 triplets

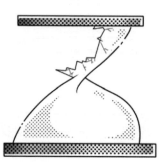

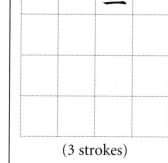

(3 strokes)

注 二 (4)
　王 (15)
　五 (6)

学 The *three* parts of a sandwich: two slices and its contents.

特 参 (hom)

---

6 (4級)

FIVE

五

ゴ
- ご 五 five (the number)
- ご ひゃく 五百 five hundred
- ご がつ 五月 May
- ご かん 五感 the five senses
- ご じゅうおん 五十音 japanese syllabary

いつ(つ)
- いつ 五つ five (items)
- いつか 五日 the fifth (day)

一 丁 石 五

(4 strokes)

注 玉 (16)

学 *Five* minutes of your time.

特 伍 (alt)

7

SIX

(4級)

(4 strokes)

ロク
六 ろく six (the number)
六千 ろくせん six thousand
六月 ろくがつ June
六角 ろっかく hexagon
第六感 だいろっかん sixth sense

むっ(つ)
六つ むっ six (items)

むい
六日 むいか the sixth (day)

特 陸(hom)

学 With the hat so low, you can only see two of the spider legs; the other *six* are under the hat.

注 売 (110)

8

SEVEN

(4級)

(2 strokes)

シチ
七 しち seven (the number)
七月 しちがつ July
七五三 しちごさん Shichigosan (festival)

なな(つ)
七 なな seven (the number)
七万 ななまん seventy thousand
七つ なな seven (items)

Special
七日 なのか the seventh (day)

特

学 The gymnast trains *seven* days a week.

注 七 (no Jōyō)
士 (4th)

Exercises　練習

1. Develop the stroke order of the following kanji

上									
下									
五									

2. Choose the correct reading for each kanji or kanji combination.

a) 三月 三日は、お誕生日ですか？

Is March, the third, your birthday?

三月：　　1．ざんつき　　2．ざんがつ　　3．さんがつ　　4．みつがつ

三日：　　1．みっか　　　2．さんにち　　3．さんび　　　4．そら

b) ベッドの上に二つの枕がある。

There are two pillows on the bed.

上：　　　1．じょう　　　2．しょう　　　3．うえ　　　　4．した

二つ：　　1．ふたつ　　　2．につ　　　　3．さんつ　　　4．みつ

c) あの二人は、七月に結婚して、もうすぐ三つ子が生まれるんだって。

Those two got married in July and said they will soon have triplets.

二人：　　1．ふたじん　　2．ふたり　　　3．にり　　　　4．にじん

七月：　　1．なにがつ　　2．なのがつ　　3．なながつ　　4．しちがつ

三つ子：　1．さんつご　　2．さっつご　　3．みつご　　　4．みつこ

3. Write the kanji (one or more) and the meaning of the following words.

ごがつ	＿＿＿月＿＿＿＿	いっぽん	＿＿＿本＿＿＿＿
なのか	＿＿＿日＿＿＿＿	みっか	＿＿＿日＿＿＿＿
のぼる	＿＿＿＿＿＿＿＿	いつつ	＿＿＿＿＿＿＿＿

4. Correct either the reading or writing mistakes in the following words.

二つ	につ	二時	ふたじ	五日	ごにち
上り坂	あがりざか	下る	さがる	一五三	しちごさん
一回	いちかい	一人	いちにん	第六感	だいろくかん

Answers to exercises 練習解答

1. (Check them in the corresponding kanji tables #2, #3, and #6.)

2. a) 三月: 3 | 三日: 1 // b) 上. 3 | 二つ: 1 // c) 二人: 2 | 七月: 4 | 三つ子: 3

3. ごがつ: 五月, May | いっぽん: 一本, one (slender, long thing) | なのか: 七日, the seventh

みっか: 三日, the third | のぼる: 上る, to climb (steps) | いつつ: 五つ, five

4. 二つ ふたつ | 二時 にじ | 五日 いつか

上り坂 のぼりざか | 下がる さがる (or 下る: くだる) | 七五三 しちごさん

一回 いっかい | 一人 ひとり | 第六感 だいろっかん

Manga translation マンガ翻訳

Elder brother: Let's play hide-and-seek!

Younger brother: Yippee! You are it, ok?!

Elder: One, two, three...

Elder: ...Five, six, seven... / **Elder:** Are you ready? I'm coming!

Younger: Ready!

Younger: He, he, he... He'll never find me here!

Elder: Hum, where can he be? Not under the futon...

Elder: On top of the fridge, not here either...

Elder: Ah! Maybe...

Elder: You idiot! really! Imagine hiding under the foot warmer...

Younger: I... I can't breathe...

New elements 新しい部首

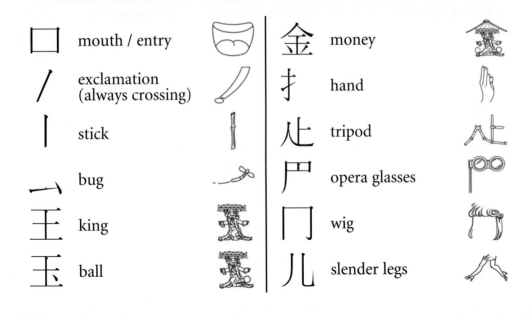

口	mouth / entry	金	money
／	exclamation (always crossing)	扌	hand
丨	stick	止	tripod
一	bug	尸	opera glasses
王	king	冂	wig
玉	ball	儿	slender legs

Lesson 2
第二課

9 (4級) — EIGHT

ハチ
はち
八 eight (the number)
はちにん
八人 eight people
はちがつ
八月 August

や(っつ)
や
八つ eight (items)
や お や
八百屋 greengrocer's

よう
ようか
八日 the eighth (day)

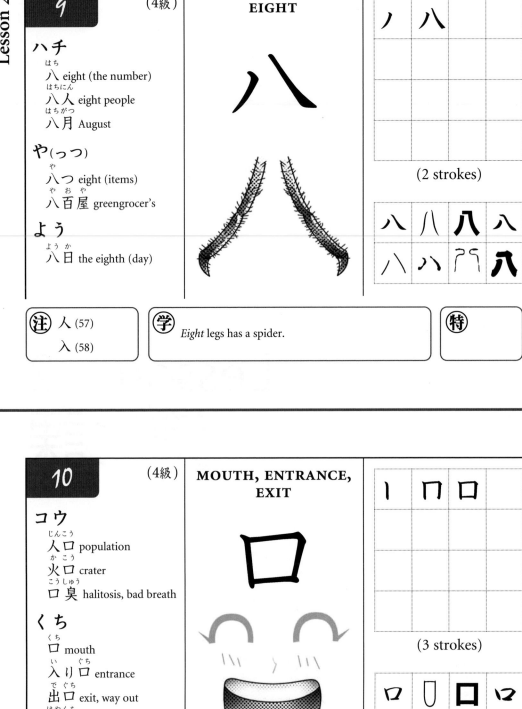

ノ 八

(2 strokes)

八 八 **八** 八
八 八 バ **八**

注 人 (57)
　　入 (58)

学 *Eight* legs has a spider.

特

10 (4級) — MOUTH, ENTRANCE, EXIT

コウ
じんこう
人口 population
かこう
火口 crater
こうしゅう
口臭 halitosis, bad breath

くち
くち
口 mouth
い　ぐち
入り口 entrance
で　ぐち
出口 exit, way out
はやくち
早口 tongue twister
くちべに
口紅 lipstick, rouge

｜ 冂 口

(3 strokes)

口 凵 **口** 冖
口 ㄴ ㅂ **口**

注 四 (11)
　　兄 (215)

学 The *mouth* is the entrance of the soul.
　Radical: 口 , 冖 or 囗

特

(5 strokes)

FOUR

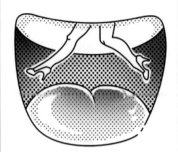

(4級) 11

シ
四角 square
四月 April
四季 the four seasons

よん / よ(っつ)
四 four (the number)
四コマ a 4-panel comic strip
四つ four (items)
四時 four o'clock
四人 four people

特 三 (alt)

学 A *four*-year old boy, who runs up and down and talks a mile a minute. What is it? A mouth with slender legs.

注 口 (10)
西 (200)

(5 strokes)

STONE, ROCK

(2級) 12

セキ
石炭 coal
石油 petroleum
宝石 precious stone; jewel

コク
石 (unit of volume = 47.6 gal)

いし
石 stone
小石 pebble
石田 Ishida (surname)

特

学 The slice you're putting in your mouth... is *rock* hard!
Radical: 石, 石 or 石

注 右 (29)
若 (6th)

13 (4級)

INSIDE, CENTER, CHINA

(4 strokes)

チュウ
中心 center
中国 China
中東 Middle East
中世 Middle Ages

なか
中 center, inside
真ん中 right in the middle
背中 the back
中田 Nakata (surname)

注 虫 (14)

学 If you don't want to open your mouth for the doctor to look *inside*, he'll put a stick in the center, as if you were a crocodile!

特

14 (2級)

BUG, INSECT

(6 strokes)

チュウ
昆虫 insect
害虫 harmful insect
幼虫 larva

むし
虫 insect, bug
毛虫 caterpillar
泣き虫 crybaby
虫歯 decayed tooth, a cavity

注 丈 (4th)
中 (13)

学 The stick keeps the mouth open. With your mouth open, a *bug* might get in!
Radical: 虫

特 蟲 (old)

KING

一 丁 干 王

(4 strokes)

(2級)

オウ

王 (おう) king
王様 (おおさま) king, monarch
国王 (こくおう) king of the country
王室 (おうしつ) royal family
女王 (じょおう) queen
王朝 (おうちょう) dynasty
王座 (おうざ) throne
王冠 (おうかん) crown

(特)

(学) A *king*, crowned with open arms.

(注) 玉 (16)
主 (3rd)

BALL, JEWEL

一 丁 干 王
玉

(5 strokes)

(2級)

ギョク

宝玉 (ほうぎょく) gem, jewel
玉露 (ぎょくろ) *gyokuro* green tea
紅玉 (こうぎょく) ruby

たま

玉 (たま) ball
玉ねぎ (たま) onion
目玉 (めだま) eyeball
玉子 (たまご) egg
金玉 (きんたま) testicle(s)

(特)

(学) The king's favorite pastime is playing *ball*.
Radical: 王

(注) 五 (6)
王 (15)
主 (3rd)

17 (4級)

METAL, GOLD, MONEY, FRIDAY

キン
きんぞく
金属 metal
きんようび
金曜日 Friday
じゅんきん
純金 pure gold
きんか
金貨 gold coin

かね
かね
お金 money
かねも
金持ち rich
かねだ
金田 Kaneda (surname)

(8 strokes)

注 宝 (6th)

全 (3rd)

学 The king keeps his "balls" (and his *money* and gold) under the umbrella.
Radical: 金 or 金

特

---

18 (4級)

HAND

シュ
はくしゅ
拍手 handclapping
かしゅ
歌手 singer
しゅだん
手段 means, measures

て
て
手 hand
てくび
手首 wrist
ひだりて
左手 left hand
てぶくろ
手袋 glove
て　　　はい
手に入る to obtain,
　　　　　　to come by

(4 strokes)

注 千 (28)

毛 (216)

学 Three fingers in the *hand*.
Radical: 扌

特

32

19

(7 strokes)

FOOT, LEG, TO BE ENOUGH

(4級)

ソク
えんそく
遠足 excursion

あし
あし
足 foot, leg
て あし
手足 hands and feet
あしおと
足音 sound of footsteps

た(りる/す/る)
た
足りる to be enough
た
足す to add
た
足る to be enough

特

 A tripod is to the camera what *feet / legs* are to the mouth.
Radical: 𧘇 or 足

注 定 (3rd)

20

(4 strokes)

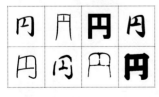

CIRCLE, YEN

(4級)

エン
えん
円 yen, circle
じゅうえん
十円 ten yen
えんだか
円高 strong yen
(exchange rate)
えん しゅう
円周 circumference

まる(い)
まる
円い round, circular

特 圓 (old)

学 The *yen* it costs to belong to the *circle* of friends of the opera!

注 門 (132)
巴 (not Jōyō)

しまった…足が…

虫は大嫌い～っ!!

例の純金の像が手に入ったら、四千万円…

いや、八千万円で売れるかもしれない…

間違いない…その真ん中の像、クラカオ王の像だ!

おめでとう! あんたは偽物の像のトリックにかかった千番目の奴だぞ!

い…石の玉!?

あっ、あそこか…出口だ!

カラガラガラガラ

ドドド

Exercises 練習

1. Develop the stroke order of the following kanji.

虫							
玉							
手							
足							

2. Choose the correct reading for each kanji or kanji combination.

a) あの歌手は王様と同じぐらいお金がもっているんですって。

They say that singer has as much money as the king.

歌手: 　1．かしゅう　　2．かて　　　　3．かで　　　　4．かしゅ

王様: 　1．おさま　　　2．おざま　　　3．おうさま　　4．おうざま

お金: 　1．おきん　　　2．おかね　　　3．あかね　　　4．あきん

b) 玉ねぎを口に入れると、すぐ吐きそうになるよ。

The moment I put onion into my mouth, I immediately feel like vomiting.

玉ねぎ: 1．おうねぎ　　2．おねぎ　　　3．きょぐねぎ　4．たまねぎ

口: 　　1．ぐち　　　　2．くち　　　　3．こ　　　　　4．こう

c) 十円ください。それで足りるから。

Give me ten yen, please. That should be enough.

十円: 　1．じゅえん　　2．じゅいん　　3．じゅうえん　4．じゅうまる

足りる: 1．あしりる　　2．たりる　　　3．たらりる　　4．そくりる

3. Write the kanji (one or more) and the meaning of the following words.

てあし	_____ _____	きんたま	_____ _____
かねもち	<u>持ち</u> _____	いし	_____ _____
よにん	<u>人</u> _____	まるい	_____ _____

4. Correct either the reading or writing mistakes in the following words.

口人	よにん	石油	いしゆ	火口	かぐち
中	むし	毛虫	けちゅう	王ねぎ	たまねぎ
玉子	たまこ	全曜日	きんようび	円るい	まるい

Answers to exercises 練習解答

1. (Check them in the corresponding kanji tables #14, #16, #18, and #19.)

2. a) 歌手: 4 | 王様: 3 | お金: 2 // b) 玉ねぎ: 4 | 口: 2 // c) 十円: 3 | 足りる: 2

3. てあし: 手足, hands and feet | きんたま: 金玉, testicle | かねもち: 金持ち, rich

いし: 石, stone | よにん: 四人, four people | まるい: 円い, round, circular

4. 四人 よにん | 石油 せきゆ | 火口 かこう

虫 むし | 毛虫 けむし | 玉ねぎ たまねぎ

玉子 たまご | 金曜日 きんようび | 円~~子~~い まるい

Manga translation マンガ翻訳

Explorer: Damn! My leg... / **Explorer:** I hate bugs!!

Explorer: If I come by that famous pure gold statuette, I'll be able to sell it for forty... No, for eighty million yen!

Explorer: There's no doubt... That one, right in the middle, is king Kula-Kao's statue!

Explorer: A stone ball?!

Sound of the stone: Rumble rumble rumble

Explorer (offscreen): Oh, there... The way out!

Sound of footsteps: Stomp stomp stomp

Savage chief: Congratulations! You are sucker number one thousand who has fallen for the fake idol trick!

Handclapping: Clap clap clap

New elements 新しい部首

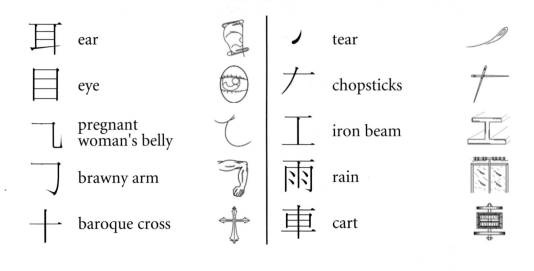

耳	ear		ノ	tear	
目	eye		大	chopsticks	
乃	pregnant woman's belly		工	iron beam	
丁	brawny arm		雨	rain	
十	baroque cross		車	cart	

Lesson 3
第三課

21 (4級) — EAR

ジ

じ もく
耳目 ears and eyes
ない じ
内耳 inner ear
じ かい
耳介 auricle
じ び か
耳鼻科 otorhinology

みみ

みみ
耳 ear
はやみみ
早耳 quick-eared
みみせん
耳栓 earplugs
みみくそ
耳糞 earwax

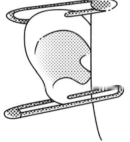

一 厂 厅 耳
耳 耳

(6 strokes)

注 目 (22)
　 日 (33)
　 百 (38)

学 The ear of this rockstar is pierced with safety pins on top and bottom.
Radical: 耳 .

特

---

22 (4級) — EYE, (ORDINAL)

モク

もくてき
目的 aim
ちゅうもく
注目 attention
もくじ
目次 index

め

め
目 eye
めだま
目玉 eyeball
めざ
目覚める to wake up
おおめ み
大目で見る overlook
いちばんめ
一番目 the first

丨 冂 冃 目
目

(5 strokes)

注 自(173), 日 (33)
　 貝 (23), 見 (24)

学 Pictogram of an *eye*.
Radical: 目 , 𠬝 or 目.

特

38

23

(7 strokes)

**SHELLFISH,
SEASHELL, CONCH**

（2級）

カイ
貝 shellfish, clam
_{かい}
貝殻 seashell
_{かいがら}
貝類 shellfish
_{かいるい}
真珠貝 pearl oyster
_{しんじゅがい}
鳥貝 cockle
_{とりがい}
二枚貝 bivalve shellfish
_{にまいがい}

特 蜆 (alt)

学 Be careful: if you scare it, the *shellfish* with the large eye will shake its legs.

注 見 (24)
目 (22)
自 (173)

24

(7 strokes)

**TO SEE, TO LOOK,
TO SHOW**

（4級）

ケン
見学 to study by observation
_{けんがく}
発見 discovery
_{はっけん}

み（る/える/せる）

見る to see, to look
_み
見える to be visible
_み
見せる to show
_み
見つける to find
_み
見本 sample
_{み ほん}
花見 blossoms festival
_{はな み}

特

学 Legs you can't help *looking* at.

注 目 (22)
貝 (23)

25 （4級）

NINE

ク
く
九 nine (the number)
く がつ
九月 September

キュウ
きゅう
九 nine (the number)
きゅうしゅう
九州 Kyūshū island

ここの（つ）
ここの
九つ nine (items)
ここの か
九日 the ninth (day)

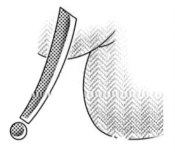

ノ 九

(2 strokes)

九 八 **九** 九
九 九 九 **九**

注 力 (26)

学 Wow, what a belly! She's *nine* months pregnant.

特

---

26 （3級）

STRENGTH

リキ
りき し
力士 sumo wrestler
じんりきしゃ
人力車 rickshaw

リョク
がくりょく
学力 scholastic ability
のうりょく
能力 ability, capacity

ちから
ちから
力 strength
ちから し ごと
力仕事 physical labor

コ 力

(2 strokes)

力 刀 **力** 力
力 力 ㇆ **力**

注 刀 (93)
　九 (25)

学 That's *strong*!!

特

27

TEN (4級)

一 十

(2 strokes)

ジュウ
十 *juu* ten
十月 *juugatsu* November
十分 *juubun* enough
十字架 *juujika* a crucifix, a cross

とお
十 *too* ten
十日 *tooka* the tenth (day)

特 拾 (hom)

学 The cross of the *Ten* Commandments.
Radical: †

注 千 (28)

28

THOUSAND (4級)

一 二 千

(3 strokes)

セン
千 *sen* a thousand
千円 *sen'en* a thousand yens
千人 *sennin* a thousand people
千年 *sennen* millennium

ち
千葉 *chiba* Chiba city
千鳥 *chidori* plover

特 韆 (alt)

学 The *thousand*-year-old cross cures thousands of sick people who cry before it.

注 十 (27)

29 (4級)

RIGHT

ウ
右折 right turn
右翼 right wing

ユウ
左右 left and right, to control

みぎ
右 right
右腕 right arm
右手 right hand

ノ ナ ナ 右
右

(5 strokes)

 石 (12)
若 (6th)

 To take the chopsticks to our mouth we use the *right* hand...

特

---

30 (4級)

LEFT

サ
左折 left turn
左翼 left wing
左方 left part
右往左往 to run around

ひだり
左 left
左手 left hand
左利き left-handed

一 ナ ナ 左
左

(5 strokes)

 The order of the first two strokes is different from 右.

 ...because, if we use the *left* hand, we will find an unhealthy iron beam.

特

42

31

(8 strokes)

RAIN

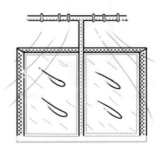

(4級)

ウ
うりょう
雨量 rainfall

あめ
あめ
雨 rain
おおあめ
大雨 downpour
あめ ふ
雨が降る to rain

あま
あまぐも
雨雲 rain cloud
あまみず
雨水 rainwater

学 Look through the window to see the *rain* fall.
Radical: 雨

注 再 (3rd)

43

32

(7 strokes)

CAR, CART, VEHICLE

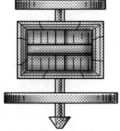

(4級)

シャ
じどうしゃ
自動車 automobile
しゃたい
車体 chassis / body (of a car)
でんしゃ
電車 train
じてんしゃ
自転車 bicycle
ふうしゃ
風車 windmill

くるま
くるま
車 car, cart
は ぐるま
歯車 gears
くるま いす
車椅子 wheelchair

学 Pictogram of an ancient *car*: an oxen cart.
Radical: 車 .

注 早 (39)
東 (199)
重 (3rd)

Exercises 練習

1. Develop the stroke order of the following kanji.

耳									
右									
左									
雨									

2. Choose the correct reading for each kanji or kanji combination.

a) 左右をよく見てから、道を渡りなさい。

Carefully look right and left before crossing the road.

左右： 1．さゆう 2．うさ 3．ゆうさ 4．ゆさ

見て： 1．かいて 2．めて 3．みて 4．みみて

b) 雨の日は車が多いから、道は危ないです。

On rainy days there are many cars, so streets are dangerous.

雨： 1．まめ 2．あめ 3．あま 4．あみ

車： 1．しゃ 2．じゃ 3．ぐるま 4．くるま

c) 力を貸してくれれば、ここは大目で見てあげるよ。

If you lend me a hand, I will overlook this.

力： 1．りき 2．ちから 3．りゅく 4．りょく

大目： 1．だいもく 2．たいもく 3．おおもく 4．おおめ

3. Write the kanji (one or more) and the meaning of the following words.

かい ＿＿＿＿ ＿＿＿＿ みみ ＿＿＿＿ ＿＿＿＿

めだま ＿＿＿＿ ＿＿＿＿ みせる ＿＿＿＿ ＿＿＿＿

せんえん ＿＿＿＿ ＿＿＿＿ ここのつ ＿＿＿＿ ＿＿＿＿

4. Correct either the reading or writing mistakes in the following words.

十日	じゅうか	目耳	じもく	花貝	はなみ
自転車	じてんさ	東	くるま	大雨	おおあま
九士	りきし	左手	みぎて	右左	さゆう

Answers to exercises 練習解答

1. (Check them in the corresponding kanji tables #21, #29, #30, and #31.)

2. a) 左右: 1 | 見て: 3 // b) 雨: 2 | 車: 4 // c) 力: 2 | 大目: 4

3. かい: 貝, shellfish | みみ: 耳, ear | めだま: 目玉, eyeball

みせる: 見せる, to show | せんえん: 千円, a thousand yen | ここのつ: 九つ, nine

4. 十日 とおか | 耳目 じもく | 花見 はなみ

自転車 じてんしゃ | 車 くるま | 大雨 おおあめ

力士 りきし | 左手 ひだりて, 右手 みぎて | 左右 さゆう

Manga translation マンガ翻訳

Silly friend: Gee, rainy days are boring...

Clever friend: Hey, why don't we go looking for snails?

Silly: Good idea! I love gathering shells!

Clever: You idiot! Snails have nothing to do with shells!

Silly: Ouch! My ear!

Clever: Come on, run. We don't even need a car.

Silly: Wow, you're strong!

Clever: Open your eyes wide, and look carefully. I'm going to find 6, 9, 10... A thousand snails!

Clever: Hm?

Sound of a tentacle: Plop

Alien: On rainy days, one must certainly go to the woods to gather humans...

Clever: Stop running around and help meeeee!

New elements 新しい部首

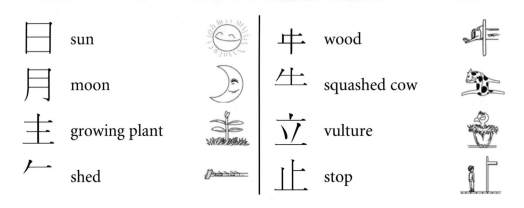

日	sun		牛	wood	
月	moon		生	squashed cow	
主	growing plant		立	vulture	
广	shed		止	stop	

Lesson 4
第四課

33 (4級)

SUN, DAY, JAPAN, SUNDAY

ニチ / ニ
にちよう び
日曜日 Sunday
にっぽん　に ほん
日本 / 日本 Japan

ジツ
きゅうじつ
休日 holiday

ひ
ひ
日 sun
あさ ひ
朝日 rising sun

か
みっ か
三日 the third (day)

 丨 冂 月 日

(4 strokes)

注 目 (22)
　 白 (37)

学 A bright *sun* says, Good *day*!
Radical: 日 , 冒 or 旦.

特

34 (4級)

MOON, MONTH, MONDAY

ゲツ
げつよう び
月曜日 Monday
に か　 げつ
二ヶ月 two months

ガツ
はちがつ
八月 August
しょう がつ
正月 New Year
じゅう に がつ
十二月 December

つき
つき
月 moon
まいつき
毎月 every month

 丿 刀 月 月

(4 strokes)

注 身 (3rd)
　 明 (227)

学 The *Moon*, queen of the night. Radical: 月 . There is another radical with the same form, but with the meaning of "flesh" (derived from 肉).

特 冃 (alt)
　 月 (alt)

35

(5 strokes)

LIFE, TO BE BORN, RAW, STUDENT

(4級)

セイ ‖ ショウ
生徒 pupil
生涯 lifetime

い (きる / かす) ‖ なま
生かす to let live
生魚 raw fish

う (まれる / む)
生まれる to be born

は (える / やす)
生える to grow, to sprout

 The tear of a plant who has been *born* into life.

 先 (41)

36

(8 strokes)

BLUE, GREEN, YOUTH

(3級)

セイ
青春 youth
青年 young person
青天 blue sky

あお (い)
青い blue
青白い pale
青空 blue sky
青信号 green traffic light

蒼 (hom)
碧 (hom)
靑 (alt)

 Blue are the plants growing on the Moon.

晴 (228)
春 (156)

37 （4級）

WHITE, CLEAR, TO CONFESS

ハク
白人 Caucasian
　はくじん
明白 clear
　めいはく

ビャク
白蓮 white lotus
　びゃくれん

しろ（い）
白い white
　しろ
白金 silver
　しろがね

しら
白髪 white / gray hair
　しらが

(5 strokes)

注 日 (33)
　百 (38)
　自 (173)

学 White are the *Sun*'s tears.
Radical: 白 .

特

38 （4級）

HUNDRED, MANY

ヒャク
百 hundred
　ひゃく
百円 a hundred yen
　ひゃくえん
百才 a hundred years
　ひゃくさい
百万 a million
　ひゃくまん
百姓 farmer, peasant
　ひゃくしょう
百貨店 department store
　ひゃっかてん
百科事典 encyclopedia
　ひゃっかじてん

(6 strokes)

注 白 (37)
　首 (174)

学 A slice of 100% natural *white*, sun-baked bread.

特

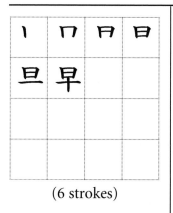

(6 strokes)

EARLY, FAST

ソウ
早春 early spring
早朝 early in the morning

サツ
早速 immediately

はや (い/める/まる)
早い early, fast
早口 tongue twister
早起き early-riser
早める to hasten

特

学 A nice sun-cross wakes up *early* in the morning.

注 草 (69)
車 (32)

(6 strokes)

YEAR

ネン
百年 a hundred years
年間 period of a year
新年 new year
年金 pension
少年 boy

とし
年 year
今年 this year
半年 half year

特

学 In a shed we keep wood for all the *year* round.

注 牛 (146)

41 (4級)

PREVIOUS, TIP, AHEAD

セン

先着 (せんちゃく) to arrive first
先頭 (せんとう) (in the) lead
先進国 (せんしんこく) developed nation
先生 (せんせい) teacher
先輩 (せんぱい) senior, *senpai*

さき

先に (さき) before
指先 (ゆびさき) fingertip
行き先 (いさき) destination

 ノ 仁 牛 生 牛 先

(6 strokes)

先 先 **先** 先
先 先 先 **先**

注 生 (36)

学 This squashed cow knows that, in a *previous* life, it was human.

特

---

42 (4級)

TO RISE, STANDING, TO SET UP

リツ

起立 (きりつ) to stand up
独立 (どくりつ) independence
私立 (しりつ) private
成立 (せいりつ) establishment
立体 (りったい) solid body

た(つ/てる)

立つ (た) to stand
立てる (た) to raise
立場 (たちば) point of view, standpoint

、 亠 广 立 立

(5 strokes)

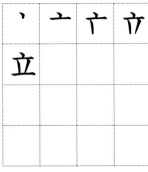

立 立 **立** 立
立 立 立 **立**

注 六 (7)

学 The gloomy vulture waits *standing...*
Radical: 立

特

(9 strokes)

SOUND

（3級）

オン
音声 voice, sound
発音 pronunciation
音符 musical note (♪)

イン
母音 vowel

おと / ね
音 sound
物音 sound, noise
本音 real (true) intention

 音 (alt)

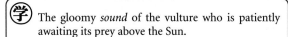 The gloomy *sound* of the vulture who is patiently awaiting its prey above the Sun.

 春 (156)
者 (3rd)

(5 strokes)

CORRECT, RIGHT

（3級）

セイ
正解 correct answer
正確 precise
正義 justice

ショウ
正午 noon
正月 New Year

ただ（しい/す）
正しい correct
正す to correct

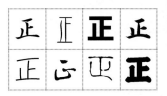

 Stop obesity! To stop eating bread is the *right* thing.

 止 (2nd)
定 (3rd)

あれ？正夫君じゃない？
久しぶり！
へえ？先生として私立学校で仕事か？さすが正夫君！
そう…今年のお正月から…
でも、どうしたの、その白髪？百才のおじいちゃんみたいだよ。まだ青年なのに…
あ、これ…
実は、最初の日に…
ははは
はあ…きっと、私の新しい生徒はいたずらを仕掛けるかも…しょうがない。
ガチャン
ん？この音…水じゃないみたいなぁ…なんだろう？
皆さん、おはよう…
ははは
ははは
ドカーン
というわけです。
わ、わかった…

Exercises 練習

1. Develop the stroke order of the following kanji.

日						
年						
先						
正						

2. Choose the correct reading for each kanji or kanji combination.

a) あなた、今年の十二月に赤^{あか}ちゃんが生まれるの。

Darling, in December of this year the baby will be born.

今年:　　1．ことし　　2．こんねん　　3．こんとし　　4．こねん

十二月:　1．じゅにげつ　2．じゅうにげつ　3．じゅにがつ　　4．じゅうにがつ

生まれる:1．いまれる　　2．なまれる　　3．うまれる　　4．はまれる

b) あの生徒の発音は正しいから、先に帰^{かえ}らせた。

That pupil's pronunciation is so correct, I've allowed him to leave before (the others).

生徒:　　1．しょうと　　2．せいと　　3．しょうとう　4．せいとう

発音:　　1．はっぽん　　2．はつおん　　3．はっぴん　　4．はついん

正しい:　1．せいしい　　2．ただしい　　3．たたしい　　4．しょうしい

先に:　　1．せんに　　2．せに　　　　3．さぎに　　　4．さきに

c) 百年もここで立って待^まっていても、キッスしないよ。

Even if you stand here waiting for a hundred years, I won't kiss you.

百年:　　1．ひょくえん　2．ひょくとし　3．ひゃくねん　4．ひゃくとし

立って:　1．たてって　　2．りって　　　3．たって　　　4．りてって

3. Write the kanji (one or more) and the meaning of the following words.

せんせい　　_____ _____　　しょうがつ　_____ _____

しろがね　　_____ _____　　はやくち　　_____ _____

4. Correct either the reading or writing mistakes in the following words.

百円	ひゃくねん	生先	せんせい	本音	ほんおん
二ヶ月	にかがつ	年金	ねきん	青年	あおどし

Answers to exercises 練習解答

1. (Check them in the corresponding kanji tables #33, #40, #41, and #44.)

2. a) 今年: 1 | 十二月: 4 | 生まれる: 3

b) 生徒: 2 | 発音: 2 | 正しい: 2 | 先に: 4 // c) 百年: 3 | 立って: 3

3. せんせい: 先生, teacher | しょうがつ: 正月, New Year

しろがね: 白金, silver | はやくち: 早口, tongue twister

4. 百円 ひゃくえん | 先生 せんせい | 本音 ほんね

二ヶ月 にかげつ | 年金 ねんきん | 青年 せいねん

Manga translation マンガ翻訳

Friend: Hey... it's Masao!

Friend (out of the bubble): It's been a long time!

Friend: What! You're working as a teacher at a private school? You're a genius!

Teacher: Well, yes... Since this New Year...

Friend: But, how come you have so much gray hair? You look like you're a hundred years old. But you're still very young...

Teacher: Well, you know... / **(offscreen)** The fact is, on my first day...

Pupils (imagination): Ha, ha, ha

Teacher (thinking): Oh, I'm sure my new pupils have a practical joke ready for me. Anyway...

Pupils (offscreen-behind the door): Quickly, hurry up!

Teacher: Good morning, everybody... / **Sound from above his head:** Claaang

Teacher (thinking): Uh? This sound... It doesn't sound like water, what can it be?

Sound of the ball: Crasssh / **Pupils (offscreen):** Ha, ha, ha, ha

Teacher: ...And that is what happened. / **Friend:** Right... I see...

New elements 新しい部首

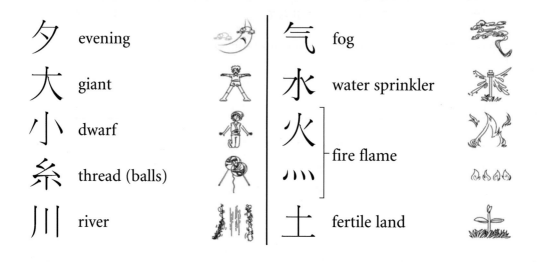

夕 evening

大 giant

小 dwarf

糸 thread (balls)

川 river

気 fog

水 water sprinkler

火
川 fire flame

土 fertile land

Lesson 5
第五課

45 (3級)

EVENING

セキ
今夕 this evening

ゆう
夕べ evening
夕方 evening
夕陽 the setting sun
夕刊 evening paper

Special
七夕 Tanabata (Festival on July, the 7th)

夕

ノ ク 夕

(3 strokes)

注 外(128)
名(46)
多(85)

学 *Evening* is when the Moon is still half covered by the mists.

特

---

46 (4級)

NAME, FAME

メイ
名刺 business card
有名な famous
名人 famous person

ミョウ
名字 surname
大名 daimyo (feudal lord)

な
名前 name
仮名 *kana* (syllabaries)

名

ノ ク 夕 夕
名 名

(6 strokes)

注 夕(45)
多(85)

学 In the evening, a mouth whispers your *name*.

特

47

(3 strokes)

BIG, UNIVERSITY

(4級)

ダイ
大学 university
大臣 minister
大丈夫 well, correct

タイ
大会 tournament
大使 ambassador

おお(きい)
大きい big
大バカ damned idiot

特

学 The giant is a *biiiig* and threatening being.
Radical: 大 or 大.

注 犬 (48)
天 (68)
太 (192)

48

(4 strokes)

DOG

(3級)

ケン
番犬 watchdog
愛犬 pet dog
秋田犬 Akita dog
アフロ犬 afro dog

いぬ
犬 dog
子犬 puppy
負け犬 a loser, a failure

特 戌 (hom)
狗 (hom)

学 A gigantic *dog* plays ball.
Radical: 犭.

 注 大 (47)
太 (192)

49 (4級)

SMALL

ショウ
少女 girl
小説 novel
小学校 elem. school

ちい(さい)
小さい small

こ
小鳥 small bird

お
小川 creek

(3 strokes)

小 小 **小** 小
小 小 氺 **小**

注 少 (86)
川 (51)
水 (53)

学 A *dwarf*, reduced to his simplest form: torso and arms.
Radical: ⺌.

特

---

50 (2級)

THREAD

シ
綿糸 cotton thread
金糸 gold thread

いと
糸 thread
毛糸 wool
絹糸 silk thread
糸口 clue, thread end

(6 strokes)

糸 糸 **糸** 糸
糸 糸 宋 **糸**

注 素 (5th)
後 (157)

学 Two balls of *thread* with their knitting needles.
Radical: 糸.

特 絲 (old)

51

RIVER （4級）

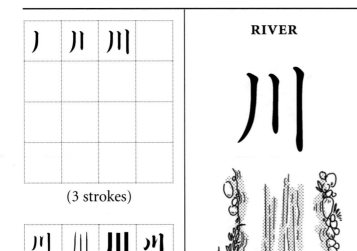

川

(3 strokes)

丿 川 川

セン
河川 rivers
<small>か せん</small>
山川 mountains and rivers
<small>さんせん</small>

かわ
川 river
<small>かわ</small>
淀川 Yodo river
<small>よどがわ</small>
ドナウ川 Danube river
<small>がわ</small>
天の川 Milky Way
<small>あま がわ</small>
滝川 river rapids
<small>たきがわ</small>
川口 Kawaguchi (surname)
<small>かわぐち</small>

（特）河 (hom)

（学）Pictogram of a flowing *river*.
Radical: 巛

（注）三 (5)
水 (53)

52

GAS, AIR, ESSENCE, SPIRIT （4級）

丿 𠂉 气 气
気 気

(6 strokes)

気

キ
空気 air, atmosphere
<small>くう き</small>
電気 electricity
<small>でん き</small>
元気 vigor, energy
<small>げん き</small>
人気 popularity
<small>にん き</small>
気に入る to like
<small>き い</small>
気のせい (just) one's
<small>き</small> imagination

ケ
寒気 the shiver, the chills
<small>さむ け</small>
吐き気 nausea
<small>は け</small>
色気 sexiness
<small>いろ け</small>

（特）氣 (old)
气 (alt)
炁 (alt)

（学）The fog is the manifestation of the *spirit* of the dead and the living.

（注）汽 (167)

53　(4級)

WATER, WEDNESDAY

スイ
海水 sea water (かいすい)
水泳 swimming (すいえい)
水分 moisture (すいぶん)
水曜日 Wednesday (すいようび)

みず
水 water (みず)
水着 swimming costume (みずぎ)
雨水 rainwater (あまみず)
水虫 athlete's foot (みずむし)

(4 strokes)

注　氷 (3rd)
　　永 (5th)

学　The water sprinkler sends water in four directions.
　　Radical: 氵 or 氺.

特

54　(4級)

FIRE, TUESDAY

カ
火口 crater (かこう)
火事 fire, conflagration (かじ)
消火器 fire extinguisher (しょうかき)
火器 firearms (かき)
火曜日 Tuesday (かようび)
火星 Mars (かせい)

ひ
火 fire (ひ)
花火 fireworks (はなび)

(4 strokes)

注　小 (49)
　　炎 (Jōyō)

学　Pictogram of *fire* (with two sparks).
　　Radical: 灬, 火, 𤉇, or 炋.

特　 伙 (alt)

55

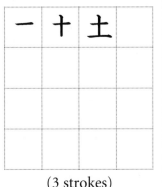

(3 strokes)

EARTH, SAND,

ド

粘土 clay (ねん ど)

土器 pottery, earthenware (ど き)

国土 national territory (こく ど)

土曜日 Saturday (ど よう び)

ト

土地 land (と ち)

つち

土 land (つち)

土色 earth-color (つちいろ)

特 圡 (alt)
　　 坔 (alt)

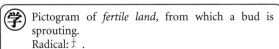
学 Pictogram of *fertile land*, from which a bud is sprouting.
Radical: 土 .

注 士 (4th)
　　上 (2)

56

(7 strokes)

RED

セキ

赤十字 Red Cross (せき じゅう じ)

赤道 equator (せき どう)

赤軍 Red Army (せき ぐん)

赤外線 infrared rays (せき がい せん)

赤飯 rice with *azuki* (せき はん)
　　 (red beans)

あか(い)

赤い red (あか)

赤字 deficit, the red (あか じ)

赤ちゃん baby (あか)

特 紅 (hom)

学 Earth cooked by *fire* is red-hot.

注 変 (4th)
　　走 (191)

Exercises 練習

1. Develop the stroke order of the following kanji.

糸								
水								
火								
赤								

2. Choose the correct reading for each kanji or kanji combination.

a) 夕べの花火を見てた子犬はとてもかわいかった。

The puppy who looked at the fireworks in the evening was very cute.

夕べ：　1．ゆうべ　　2．ゆべ　　　3．うべ　　　4．たなべ

花火：　1．はなか　　2．はなひ　　3．はなび　　4．かび

子犬：　1．こいぬ　　2．こけん　　3．しいぬ　　4．しけん

b) 聞いたことのある名前だと思ったら、有名な人だったらしいよ。

I thought I had heard that name, it turns out he's famous!

名前：　1．めいぜん　　2．みょうぜん　3．なぜん　　4．なまえ

有名：　1．ゆうみょう　2．ゆみょう　　3．ゆめい　　4．ゆうめい

c) 赤字を見ただけでも、寒気をしてしまう。

Just looking at the red (the deficit) gives me the shivers.

赤字：　1．あかし　　2．あかじ　　3．せきじ　　4．せきし

寒気：　1．さむき　　2．さむぎ　　3．さむけ　　4．さむげ

3. Write the kanji (one or more) and the meaning of the following words.

おがわ　　　_____ _____　　いとぐち　　_____ _____

あまみず　　_____ _____　　どようび　　__曜__ _____

せきじゅうじ　__字__ _____　　おおバカ　　_____ _____

4. Correct either the reading or writing mistakes in the following words.

アフロ大	アフロいぬ	太使	たいし	小い	ちいさい
小学校	しょがっこう	火事	ひじ	泳水	すいえい
土曜日	どうようび	色気	いろき	人汽	にんき

Answers to exercises 練習解答

1. (Check them in the corresponding kanji tables #50, #53, #54, and #56.)

2. 夕べ:1│花火:3│子犬:1 // b) 名前:4│有名:4 // c) 赤字:2│寒気:3

3. おがわ: 小川, creek│いとぐち: 糸口, clue, thread end│あまみず: 雨水, rainwater

どようび:土曜日, Saturday│せきじゅうじ:赤十字, Red Cross│おおバカ:大バカ, damned idiot

4. アフロ犬 アフロいぬ│大使 たいし│小さい ちいさい

小学校 しょうがっこう│火事 かじ│水泳 すいえい

土曜日 ど<del>手</del>ようび│色気 いろけ│人気 にんき

Manga translation マンガ翻訳

Text panel: One Saturday, at the time the sun was turning red as fire...

Text panel: ...Well, in short, in the evening.

Girl: What? Is it just my imagination? I heard barking coming from the river...

Barking (offscreen): Woof, woof

Girl: Oh!! Is that a small dog, in the water?!

Puppy: Woof, woof!

Girl: Poor thing, how could anybody do this to you?

Girl: Uh? What's this label?

Puppy: Woof woof

Girl: "I am Greedy." Is this the puppy's name? / **Label:** I am Greedy

Girl: It's so cute! Don't worry, from now on I'll take care of you!

Puppy: Woof, woof!

Girl (thinks): Even though he is small, he sure is "greedy!" So the name was a clue after all.

Sound of wolfing down food: gobble, gobble, gobble

Caption on the sack: Puppy Chow

New elements 新しい部首

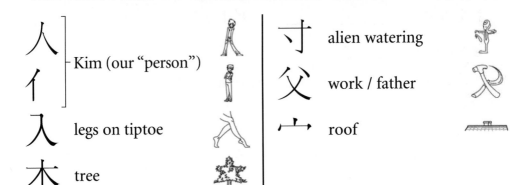

人
亻　Kim (our "person")

入　legs on tiptoe

木　tree

寸　alien watering

父　work / father

宀　roof

Lesson 6
第六課

57 (4級)

PERSON

(2 strokes)

ジン
人生 human life
日本人 Japanese (person)
外国人 foreigner

ニン
人間 human being
料理人 cook

ひと
人 person
人殺し murderer

(注) 入 (58)
　　 八 (9)

(学) Here is Kim, our *person*. (Remember, if he has company, he usually adopts the form 亻, leaving space for the other part: see *to rest* #61.)

(特)

---

58 (4級)

TO GO IN, TO PUT IN

(2 strokes)

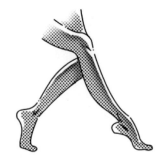

ニュウ
入学 to enter a school
入国 to enter a country
侵入 invasion

い(る／れる)
入り口 entrance
入れる to put in
入れ歯 false tooth, dentures

はい(る)
入る to go in

(注) 人 (57)

(学) A thief's legs, *going in* stealthily. (Be careful, the stroke order and direction are different from those in the kanji of *person*, #57.)

(特)

59

(4 strokes)

TREE, WOOD, THURSDAY

(4級)

モク
木曜日 Thursday
木材 wooden

ボク
木刀 wooden sword
大木 big tree

き / こ
木 tree
木登り to climb a tree
木の葉 foliage

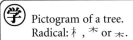 Pictogram of a tree.
Radical: 扌, 木 or 朩.

 本 (60)
休 (61)
水 (53)

60

(5 strokes)

ROOT, ORIGIN, BOOK, THIS

(4級)

ホン
本 book
本屋 bookshop
単行本 separate volume
見本 sample, specimen
日本 Japan
本日 today
本当 truth

もと
木の本 tree root

 本 (alt)

 A slice of bread is the *base* for the Christmas tree (and this year you are sure to get *books*!)

 木 (59)

61 (4級)

TO REST, TO MISS SCHOOL OR WORK

キュウ

休日 holiday
きゅうじつ

休校 cancelled school day
きゅうこう

休憩 a break
きゅうけい

連休 consecutive holidays
れんきゅう

やす(む／める／まる)

休む to rest,
やす   to take the day off

休み rest, holidays
やす

夏休み summer holidays
なつやす

休まる to be rested
やす

(6 strokes)

注 体 (190)

学 The ideal place for Kim to *rest*: in the shade of a tree.

特

---

62 (3級)

GROVE, WOODS

リン

森林 forest, grove
しんりん

林道 forest trail
りんどう

山林 mountains and woods
さんりん

はやし

林 grove, woods
はやし

松林 pine woods
まつばやし

林田 Hayashida (surname)
はやしだ

(8 strokes)

注 材 (4th)

村 (64)

学 More than one tree makes a *grove*...

特

63

(12 strokes)

FOREST

(3級)

シン
しんりん
森林 woods, forest
しんりんさいせい
森林再生 reforestation

もり
森 forest
森田 Morita (surname)
森本 Morimoto (surname)

  ...and three trees are plenty, and thus create a *forest*.

64

(7 strokes)

VILLAGE

(3級)

ソン
そんみん
村民 villagers
のうそん
農村 farm village
ぎょそん
漁村 fishing village
しちょうそん
市町村 cities, towns, and villages
そんちょう
村長 village mayor

むら
むら
村 village
むらびと
村人 villager
にいむら
新村 Niimura (surname)

 邨 (alt) An alien *village* is full of trees, watered and looked after by the aliens. 林 (62) 村 (4th)

65 (4級)

SCHOOL, TO CHECK

コウ

学校 school
(がっこう)
校長 school principal
(こうちょう)
登校 to attend school
(とうこう)
校内 school grounds
(こうない)
高校生 high school
(こうこうせい)　　student
校訂 revision
(こうてい)
校正刷り proofreading
(こうせい ず)

一 十 オ 木
オ 朽 朽 朽
校 校

(10 strokes)

 枝 (5th)

 The Mexican *school* of lumbering teaches you how to fell trees using the sickle and the hammer.

特

---

66 (3級)

TEXT, WRITING

ブン

文章 sentence
(ぶんしょう)
作文 composition
(さくぶん)
文化 culture
(ぶんか)
文明 civilization
(ぶんめい)

モン

注文 order
(ちゅうもん)
* 文字 letter, character
(もじ)

ふみ

矢文 letter tied to an arrow
(やぶみ)

、 一 ナ 文

(4 strokes)

 父 (212)
交 (213)
又 (Jōyō)

 The Mexican hat characterizes the religious person devoted to *writing*.

特

67 （4級）

SKY, AIR, EMPTY

(8 strokes)

クウ
空気 air
空港 airport

そら ‖ から
空 sky
空っぽ empty
空手 karate

あ（く／ける）‖ す（く）
空き家 vacant house
お腹が空いた I'm hungry

学 Houses in the *sky* are not only strong and made of iron bars like ours, but they also have beautiful, slender legs running around!

注 室 (126)

68 （3級）

SKY, HEAVEN

(4 strokes)

テン
天空 sky, firmament
天地 heaven and earth
天文学 astronomy
天気 weather
天使 angel
天国 Kingdom of Heaven
天皇 Emperor of Japan

あめ／あま
天の川 Milky Way

学 Kim likes bread: give him two slices and he'll be in *heaven*.

注 大 (47)
矢 (233)
夫 (4th)

ある日、突然……天空から死神のようなUFOが降りてきました。

人間どもよ！明日は地球の最後の日だ!!

きゃ～!!侵略される!!

くり返す……

次の日、人々は仕事や学校を休んだり、都市や村から逃げたりしました。

森林の木の間に入って隠れた人もいました。

そして……

今日は最後の日だ！

ゴゴゴゴ

どわ～!!文明の終わりだ!!

安売り！

今日は地球でのバーゲンの最後の日で、今なら50%の値引きになります！

本当に安いですよ！

Exercises 練習

1. Develop the stroke order of the following kanji.

入									
本									
村									
天									

2. Choose the correct reading for each kanji or kanji combination.

a) 日本人は休みが少ないと言われています。本当ですか？

They say the Japanese have few holidays. Is it true?

日本人： 1．ひほんじん 2．にほんにん 3．にほんひと 4．にほんじん

休み： 1．きゅうみ 2．きゅうひ 3．やすみ 4．やすめみ

b) 天気がいいから、森林に入って、散歩しない？

Since the weather is fine, why don't we go in the woods for a walk?

天気： 1．てんき 2．でんき 3．あまき 4．あめき

森林： 1．りしん 2．りんしん 3．しりん 4．しんりん

入って： 1．にゅうって 2．はいって 3．いれって 4．にゅって

c) 日本の本屋さんって天国だ！

Bookshops in Japan are a paradise!

本屋： 1．きや 2．ぎや 3．ほんや 4．ほや

天国： 1．てんろく 2．てんごく 3．あまこく 4．あまごく

3. Write the kanji (one or more) and the meaning of the following words.

きゅうこう ＿＿＿＿ ＿＿＿＿ やすまる ＿＿＿＿ ＿＿＿＿

むらびと ＿＿＿＿ ＿＿＿＿ からて ＿＿＿＿ ＿＿＿＿

ほんみょう ＿＿＿＿ ＿＿＿＿ じんせい ＿＿＿＿ ＿＿＿＿

4. Correct either the reading or writing mistakes in the following words.

休日	きゅうび	森木	もりもと	文字	ぶんじ
空港	くこう	空き家	すきや	天地	てんし
日本	ほんじつ	木曜日	ぼくようび	人学	にゅうがく

Answers to exercises 練習解答

1. (Check them in the corresponding kanji tables #58, #60, #64, and #68.)

2. a) 日本人: 4 | 休み: 3 // b) 天気: 1 | 森林: 4 | 入って: 2 // c) 本屋: 3 | 天国: 2

3. きゅうこう: 休校, cancelled school day | やすまる: 休まる, to be rested | むらびと: 村人, villager | からて: 空手, karate | ほんみょう: 本名, real name | じんせい: 人生, human life

4. 休日 きゅうじつ | 森本 もりもと | 文字 | もじ

空港 くうこう | 空き家 あきや | 天地 てんち

日本 にほん(or 本日 ほんじつ) | 木曜日 | もくようび | 入学 にゅうがく

Manga translation マンガ翻訳

Text panel: One day, suddenly... / UFOs came down from the sky like angels of death.

UFO: Human beings! Tomorrow will be the Earth's last day!

People: Uaahhh!! We are being invaded!!

UFO: We repeat...

Text panel: The next day, people missed work and school, and ran away from villages and cities. / **Text panel:** There were even people who went in the woods and took refuge among the trees. / **Text panel:** Then...

UFO: Today is the last day!!

People: Uaahhh!! This is the end of civilization!! / **Sound of descent:** Fwooosssh

Alien: Today is the last day of sales on the Earth, and we have half-price offers!

Alien 2: Really cheap!

Flag: Sales

New elements 新しい部首

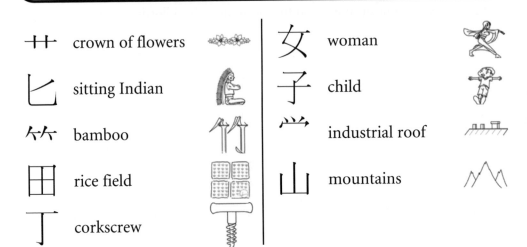

十十	crown of flowers		女	woman	
ヒ	sitting Indian		子	child	
竹	bamboo		丷丷	industrial roof	
田	rice field		山	mountains	
丁	corkscrew				

Lesson 7
第七課

69 (2級)

GRASS

ソウ
そうげん
草原 prairie
ざっそう
雑草 weeds
かいそう
海草 seaweed
そうあん
草案 (rough) draft

くさ
く さ
草 grass
く さ
草サッカー
soccer amateur

Special
たばこ
煙草 tobacco, cigarette(s)

一 十 サ サ
サ 芦 苩 莗
草

(9 strokes)

注 早 (39)

学 *Grass* sprouts early.
Radical: ⁺⁺.

特 草 (alt)

---

70 (4級)

FLOWER

カ
か ふん
花粉 pollen
か べん
花弁 petal
ぞう か
造花 artificial flower

はな
はな
花 flower
くさばな
草花 flowering plant
い ばな
生け花 *ikebana,* (the art)
of flower arrangement
はな み
花見 cherry blossom viewing
はな び
花火 fireworks

一 十 サ サ
ザ 花 花

(7 strokes)

花 花 **花** 花
花 芲 葄 **花**

注 化 (3rd)

学 Under a crown of flowers, Kim has made a new
friend: a sitting Indian. The *flower* symbolizes their
friendship.

特 花 (alt)
苍 (alt)
華 (hom)

71

(6 strokes)

BAMBOO

竹

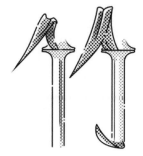

(2級)

チク
竹林 bamboo grove

たけ
竹 bamboo
竹製 made of bamboo
竹馬 stilts

Special
竹刀 bamboo sword

特

学 Pictogram of two *bamboo* canes.
Radical: 竹.

注 介 (Jōyō)

72

ー冂皿冊
田

(5 strokes)

RICE FIELD

田

(3級)

デン
乾田 dry rice field
水田 paddy
油田 oil field
炭田 coalfield

た
田 (or 田んぼ) rice field
稲田 rice field

Special
田舎 the country (≠ the city)

特

学 Pictogram of a *rice field*.
Radical: 田, 田 or 田.

注 母 (214)
毎 (218)
申 (3rd)

73 (3級)

TOWN, QUARTER

チョウ
町長 town mayor
ちょうにん
町人 townsmen
みずたちょう
水田町 village / quarter of Mizuta
しちょうそん
市町村 cities, towns, and villages

まち
まち
町 town / quarter
したまち
下町 downtown
みなとまち
港町 port town

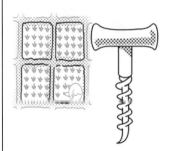

```
一 口 冊 田
田 町 町
```

(7 strokes)

町 町 **町** 町
町 西 町 **町**

注 男 (74)

学 A *town* is built where rice fields have been plucked out one by one with a corkscrew and replaced by houses.

特 街 (hom)

74 (4級)

MAN, MASCULINE

ダン
だんし
男子 boy
だんせい
男性 man, masculine
だんじょ
男女 men and women

ナン
ちょうなん
長男 eldest son

おとこ
おとこ
男 man
おとこまえ
男前 handsome, attractive
おとこのこ
男の子 boy

男

```
一 口 冊 田
田 罗 男
```

(7 strokes)

男 男 **男** 男
男 罗 罗 **男**

注 町 (73)

学 Traditionally, the *man* was the one with the physical strength to work the fields.

特 偭 (alt)

75

WOMAN, FEMININE

(4級)

(3 strokes)

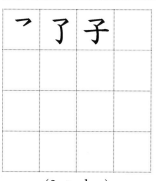

ジョ
女性 woman, feminine
女王 queen
少女 girl

ニョ / ニョウ
女房 wife
天女 celestial nymph

おんな / め
女 woman
女神 goddess

特 | 学 Pictogram of a court *woman*. Radical: 女, 女 or 女. | 文 (66)

76

CHILD, SON, DAUGHTER

(4級)

(3 strokes)

シ
女子 girl
母子 mother and child
弟子 disciple
孔子 Confucius
電子 electron

こ
子供 child, kid, baby
息子 son
正子 Masako (woman's name)

特 | 学 Pictogram of a *child* playing. Radical: 子, 子 or 子. | 了 (Jōyō) 字 (77)

77 (3級)

LETTER, CHARACTER

ジ

字 letter
文字 letter, character
漢字 kanji
ローマ字 rōmaji, Roman alphabet
数字 numbers
習字 calligraphy
赤字 deficit, the red
名字 surname
字体 letter type

(6 strokes)

注 子 (76)
　 学 (78)

学 The boy stays home (under a roof) when he starts learning Japanese language *characters*.

特

82

78 (4級)

TO LEARN, EDUCATION

ガク

学生 student
学校 school
大学 university
文学 literature
化学 chemistry
学力 learning ability
入学試験 college entrance exam

まな(ぶ)

学ぶ to learn

(8 strokes)

注 字 (77)

学 The boy *learns* under the school's industrial roof.

特 學 (old)
　 孝 (alt)

79

MOUNTAIN

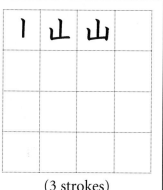

（3 strokes）

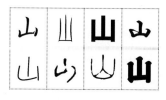

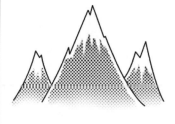

サン / ザン

山脈 <ruby>さん<rt></rt></ruby>みゃく mountain range
登山 とざん mountain climbing
火山 かざん volcano
下山 げざん going down a mountain
富士山 ふじさん Mount Fuji

やま

山 やま mountain
岩山 いわやま rocky mountain
東山 ひがしやま Mount Higashi

  Pictogram of *mountains*. Be careful with the stroke order: first the summit then, the base.
Radical: 山 , 山 or 山.

 土 (55)

80

TO COME OUT, TO TAKE OUT

（5 strokes）

シュツ

外出する がいしゅつ to go out
出発 しゅっぱつ departure

で(る / かける)

出る で to go (or come) out
出かける で to go out, leave
出来る でき to be able to

だ(す)

出す だ to take out
思い出す おも だ to remember

  From other mountains, new ones *come out*.

 生 (35)

Exercises 練習

1. Develop the stroke order of the following kanji.

草									
竹									
女									
出									

2. Choose the correct reading for each kanji or kanji combination.

a) うちの<u>女房</u>は<u>文学</u>と<u>生け花</u>が好きなんだ。

My wife likes literature and ikebana.

女房：　　1．にょぼ　　　2．にょうぼ　　　3．じょうぼう　4．にょうぼう

文学：　　1．だいがく　　2．ぶんがく　　　3．だいらく　　4．ぶんらく

生け花：1．いけはな　　2．いけばな　　　3．いけか　　　4．いきけばな

b) 「<u>子供</u>は<u>竹刀</u>で<u>遊</u>んではいかん！」と<u>長男</u>はお父さんに<u>叱</u>られた。

"Children must not play with a shinai!," the eldest son was scolded by his father.

子供　　1．ことも　　　2．こども　　　　3．しとも　　　4．しども

長男：　1．ながだん　　2．ながなん　　　3．ちょうだん　4．ちょうなん

c) <u>田舎</u>の<u>男女</u>はね、<u>長生</u>きするんだって！

They say men and women in the country live longer!

田舎：　　1．いしゃ　　　2．でんしゃ　　　3．たなか　　　4．いなか

男女：　　1．だんじょ　　2．だんじょう　　3．なんじょ　　4．なんじょう

3. Write the kanji (one or more) and the meaning of the following words.

ちくりん　　_____ _____　　　したまち　　_____ _____

おとこまえ　_____ _____　　　じょおう　　_____ _____

あかじ　　　_____ _____　　　がっこう　　_____ _____

4. Correct either the reading or writing mistakes in the following words.

学なぶ	まなぶ	花見	はなび	田ぼ	たんぼ
煙草	たばくさ	町人	まちひと	電子	でんこ
富士山	ふじやま	出発	しゅぱつ	ローマ子	ローマじ

Answers to exercises 練習解答

1. (Check them in the corresponding kanji tables #69, #71, #75, and #80.)

2. a) 女房: 4 | 文学: 2 | 生け花: 2 // b) 子供: 2 | 長男: 4 // c) 田舎: 4 | 男女: 1

3. ちくりん: 竹林, bamboo grove | したまち: 下町, downtown | おとこまえ: 男前, handsome, attractive

じょおう: 女王, queen | あかじ: 赤字, deficit, the red | がっこう: 学校, school

4. 学ぶ まなぶ | 花見 はなみ | 田んぼ たんぼ | 煙草 たばこ | 町人 ちょうにん | 電子 でんし | 富士山 ふじさん | 出発 しゅっぱつ | ローマ字 ローマじ

Manga translation マンガ翻訳

Girl: Gee, the university entrance exam is awful, just, horrible!

Girl: Just a minute... What if I take a break?

Girl: Indeed, nature is wonderful!

Girl: Getting out of town, and going for a walk in the mountain can clear your head quite a bit.

Girl: The perfume of wild flowers... Bamboo, rice fields...

Onomatopoeia of sniffing: Snif, snif

Girl: ...and, in the mountain, you can take an open-air bath. What happiness!

Curtain: Women Men @

Girl: Wow! What's that symbol? Children? To turn around? Internet?

Voice (offscreen): Hello, young girl... You look like you are at a loss, come here...

Onomatopoeia all over the panel: Blah blah blah blah

Girl (thinking): N...Now I understand... It was the symbol for "Boring grannies..."

Review of Grade 1

小学校一年生 まとめ問題

Review Grade 1 　一年生・まとめ問題

1. Link the kanji with their corresponding *kun'yomi* and *on'yomi* readings.

1.	みぎ	下	カ/ゲ
2.	ふみ	玉	キュウ
3.	はや(い)	九	サッ
4.	なま	右	ショウ
5.	な	生	ミョウ
6.	つち	早	ユウ
7.	たま	立	テン
8.	た(てる)	名	ギョク
9.	した	土	ド
10.	ここの	文	モン
11.	おと	天	リツ
12.	あめ	音	オン

2. Write the kanji missing in the following text.

_____の_____で_____んでいた。_____も_____も震えていて、歩けなかった。宝くじが当たるなんて... お_____のことをあまり気にしない彼女のような_____性は、これからどうすればいいんだろう？「穴があれば_____りたい」と本当に思った。新しい家も_____も買えたことは買えたけど、それで幸せになれるかどうかはね...

She was resting in the woods. Her hands and feet trembling, she could not walk. She had won the lottery! What was she going to do, a woman like her, who had never cared about money? She sincerely thought: "Earth, open and swallow me up." She could buy a new house and a new car, of course, but who knows if that would make her happy...

_____どもの頃からやりたかったのは_____さい_____に引っ越し、_____ _____ _____で_____ _____を教えることだった。_____に囲まれた、_____ _____以下のところを探し、いい_____と結婚し、きらいな _____ちゃんが_____まれたら、きっと幸せになれると思った。大事な _____ が_____人か_____人いれば_____分だと。

Since she was a little girl, she had wanted to move to a small village, and teach literature at a school. She would look for a place surrounded by mountains, with less than a hundred people, she would marry a good man, and a beautiful baby would be born: she could certainly be happy this way. In life, having one or two important persons is enough.

3. Choose the correct reading for each kanji or kanji combination.

a) 日本の六月と言えば、雨ばっかりだ。早く終わってほしい！

June in Japan has only one thing: rain. I want it to finish soon!

日本：　1．にき　　　2．にほん　　　3．にちき　　　4．にちほん

六月： 　1．ろくがつ　2．ろっがつ　　3．ろっつき　　4．むつき

雨：　　1．あま　　　2．あみ　　　　3．あめ　　　　4．う

早く：　1．さっく　　2．ささく　　　3．はやく　　　4．はく

b) 火事になった地域の村長たちは森林再生を実行しました。

The village mayors of the area where the fire broke out carried out the reforestation plan.

火事：　1．ひし　　　2．ひじ　　　3．かし　　　　4．かじ

村長：　1．むらなが　2．むろなが　3．そんちょう　4．そうちょう

森林：　1．しんりん　2．りんしん　3．りしん　　　4．しりん

c) できていないけど、草案ならあるよ。文字が気に入るかどうか...

It's not finished yet, but I have a draft. I wonder if you'll like my writing...

草案：　1．たばん　　2．すさん　　3．すさあん　　4．そうあん

文字：　1．もんじ　　2．もじ　　　3．ぶんし　　　4．ぶんじ

入る：　1．はいる　　2．はる　　　3．いる　　　　4．あいる

4. Choose the correct kanji for each reading.

a) たなばたってロマンチックじゃない？しちがつだったよね？それとも、くがつ？

Isn't Tanabata romantic? Was it in July? Or in September?

たなばた：　1．九夕　　2．七夕　　3．九多　　4．七多

しちがつ：　1．十月　　2．八月　　3．七月　　4．七夕

くがつ：　　1．方月　　2．九月　　3．力月　　4．刀月

b) ごひゃくえん だしてよ、このケチ！かね 持ちなのに！

Take out five hundred yen, you miser! Come on, you are filthy rich!

ごひゃくえん：1．五白円　2．五日円　3．五百円　4．語百円

だして：　　1．下して　2．出して　3．山して　4．生して

かね持ち：　1．玉持ち　2．王持ち　3．全持ち　4．金持ち

c) はなみやらない？このあおぞらをみてよ！せっかくのきゅうじつだし...

Do you want to come to a cherry blossom viewing party? Look at the bright blue sky! And it's a holiday too...

はなみ：　　1．化目　2．化火　3．花見　4．花火

あおぞら：　1．青究　2．晴空　3．晴究　4．青空

みて：　　　1．貝て　2．見て　3．耳て　4．目て

きゅうじつ：1．本目　2．木日　3．木目　4．休日

Answers to exercises　練習解答

1.

した	下	カ／ゲ
たま	玉	ギョク
ここの	九	キュウ
みぎ	右	ユウ
なま	生	ショウ
はや(い)	早	サッ
た(てる)	立	リツ
な	名	ミョウ
つち	土	ド
ふみ	文	モン
あめ	天	テン
おと	音	オン

2.　森の中で休んでいた。手も足も震えていて、歩けなかった。宝くじが当たるなんて...お金のことをあまり気にしない彼女のような女性は、これからどうすればいいんだろう？「穴があれば入りたい」と本当に思った。新しい家も車も買えたことは買えたけど、それで幸せになれるかどうかはね...

　　　子供の頃からやりたかったのは小さい村に引っ越し、小学校で文学を教えることだった。山に囲まれた、百人以下のところを探し、いい男と結婚し、きれいな赤ちゃんが生まれたら、きっと幸せになれると思った。大事な人二人か二人がいれば十分だと。

3. a) 日本: 2｜六月: 1｜雨: 3｜早く: 3

　b) 火事: 4｜村長: 3｜森林: 1

　c) 草案: 4｜文字: 2｜入る: 3

4. a) たなばた: 2｜しちがつ: 3｜くがつ: 2

　b) ごひゃくえん: 3｜だして: 2｜かねもち: 4

　c) はなみ: 3｜あおぞら: 4｜みて: 2｜きゅうじつ: 4

New elements 新しい部首

米 rice 　　歩 wise old man

父 athlete 　　与 crouching lookout

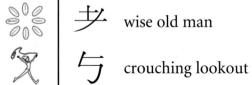

Grade　2
小学校二年生

Lesson　　8
第八課

81   (2級)

RICE, AMERICA

ベイ

米国 U.S.

べいこく

米価 rice price

べいか

日米 Japan and U.S.

にちべい

南米 South America

なんべい

こめ

米 rice (raw)

こめ

米屋 rice dealer

こめや

米粒 grain of rice

こめつぶ

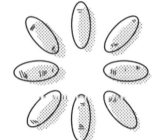

丶	丷	丷	半
半	米		

(6 strokes)

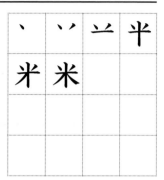

注 氷 (3rd)

来 (135)

永 (5th)

学 Pictogram of grains of *rice*.

Radical: 米 .

特

92

---

82   (3級)

NUMBER, TO COUNT

スウ

数字 figure, number

すうじ

手数 trouble, problems

てすう

数ヶ月 several months

すうかげつ

数学 mathematics

すうがく

人数 number of people

にんずう

かず

数多く great number (of)

かずおお

かぞ(える)

数える to count

かぞ

丶	丷	丷	半
米	米	娄	娄
娄	娄	娄	数
数			

(13 strokes)

注 教 (84)

学 The *number* one athlete eats rice lovingly planted by a woman.

特 數 (alt)

83 — TO THINK, TO CONSIDER (3級)

一	十	土	耂
耂	考		

(6 strokes)

コウ
- 思考 thought, idea (しこう)
- 考証 historical investigation (こうしょう)
- 参考 reference (さんこう)
- 考案 plan, idea (こうあん)
- 考慮する to consider, to bear in mind (こうりょ)

かんが（える）
- 考える to think (かんが)
- 考え出す to have an idea (かんが・だ)
- 考え事 concern (かんが・ごと)

 攷 (alt)

学 The wise old man wearing the ribbon of knowledge is now concentrated, *thinking* about the cosmos, while the lookout takes care that nobody bothers him.

注 孝 (6th)　者 (3rd)

---

84 — TO TEACH, TO EDUCATE, RELIGION (3級)

一	十	土	耂
耂	考	孝	孝
孝	教	教	

(11 strokes)

キョウ
- 教室 classroom (きょうしつ)
- 教科 subject (きょうか)
- 教材 teaching materials (きょうざい)
- 文教 education (ぶんきょう)
- 教会 church (きょうかい)
- 仏教 Buddhism (ぶっきょう)

おし（える）
- 教える to teach (おし)
- 教え子 disciple, former student (おし・ご)

 敎 (alt)

学 The wise old man *educates* the boy so that he becomes a great athlete.

注 数 (82)

85 (4級) — MANY, MUCH

タ
- 多分 (た ぶん) probably, maybe
- 多角 (た かく) many-sided, diversified
- 多数の (た すう) various, many
- 多少 (た しょう) a little

おお(い)
- 多い (おお) many, lots of
- 多目に (おお め) large portion, extra (serving)
- 多過ぎる (おお す) too many

ノ	ク	タ	タ
多	多		

(6 strokes)

学 *Many* evenings.

特 夛 (alt)

94

86 (4級) — LITTLE, FEW

ショウ
- 少年 (しょう ねん) boy
- 少女 (しょう じょ) girl
- 少数 (しょう すう) few, minority
- 少少 (しょう しょう) a little, a few
  (**Note:** the repetition of the same kanji can also be indicated with 々 [here, 少々])

すく(ない)
- 少ない (すく) little, few (adjective)

すこ(し)
- 少し (すこ) a little, a few (adverb)

丿	小	小	少

(4 strokes)

注 小 (49)

学 *Few* times does a dwarf shed a tear; he overcomes sadness by jumping over it.

特

87

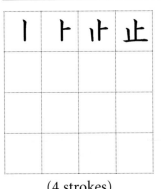

(4 strokes)

TO STOP, TO COME TO A STOP

(3級)

シ

休止 きゅうし a pause, a break
中止 ちゅうし cancellation
止水 しすい still water
禁止 きんし prohibition

と（まる/める）

止まる と to come to a stop
行き止まり いきどまり dead end
止める と to stop, to bring to a stop

特

学 Here we have a *STOP*.

注 上 (2)
　 正 (44)

88

(8 strokes)

TO WALK

(3級)

ホ

歩道 ほどう sidewalk
歩数 ほすう number of steps
進歩 しんぽ advance, progress
歩行者 ほこうしゃ pedestrian
散歩 さんぽ a walk

ある（く）

歩く ある to walk
歩き回る あるまわ to walk about
歩き出す あるだ to start walking

特

学 *Walking* is equivalent to stopping a little.

注 徒 (4th)
　 走 (191)

Exercises 練習

1. Develop the stroke order of the following kanji.

数									
考									
止									
歩									

2. Choose the correct reading for each kanji or kanji combination.

a) 白髪なら、数えられないほど多いよ。

Gray hairs? I've got so many I can't count them.

数: 1．かぞ 2．かず 3．おし 4．おしえ

多い: 1．おおい 2．おうい 3．だい 4．たい

b) 南米の教会は数が多くて、すごいの。今度あなたも行けば？

South America has many wonderful churches. Why don't you go there one day?

南米: 1．なんべ 2．なんべい 3．なんぺ 4．なんぺい

教会: 1．おしえかい 2．おしかい 3．きょかい 4．きょうかい

c) 少々 休止しましょう。こんなに歩くのがはじめてだから。

Let's take a little break. This is first time I walk so far.

少々: 1．しょうしょう 2．しょしょ 3．しょしょう 4．しょうしょ

休止: 1．くし 2．きゅし 3．きゅうし 4．くどめ

3. Write the kanji (one or more) and the meaning of the following words.

にちべい ＿＿＿＿ ＿＿＿＿ すうがく ＿＿＿＿ ＿＿＿＿

がんがえだす ＿＿＿＿ ＿＿＿＿ おしえご ＿＿＿＿ ＿＿＿＿

おおめに ＿＿＿＿ ＿＿＿＿ ちゅうし ＿＿＿＿ ＿＿＿＿

4. Correct either the reading or writing mistakes in the following words.

米屋	べいや	教字	すうじ	考え事	かんがえこと
小年	しょうねん	歩道	ほうどう	歩き回る	いきまわる
人数	ひとかず	思教	しこう	教る	おしえる

Answers to exercises 練習解答

1. (Check them in the corresponding kanji tables #82, #83, #87, and #88)

2. a) 数え：1 | 多い：1 // b) 南米：2 | 教会：4 // c) 少々：1 | 休止：3

3. にちべい：日米, Japan and U.S. | すうがく：数学, mathematics | かんがえだす：考え出す, to have an idea | おしえご： 教え子, disciple | おおめに：多目に, extra (serving) | ちゅうし：中止, cancellation

4. 米屋 こめや | 数字 すうじ | 考え事 かんがえごと | 少年 しょうねん | 歩道 ほ￢どう | 歩き回る あるきまわる | 人数 にんずう | 思考 しこう | 教える おしえる

Manga translation マンガ翻訳

Girl: Oh, it's Seiichi!

Boy: Hey, Elizabeth! Shall we go for a walk?

Boy: In fact, there's something I wanted to say to you.

Boy: Since we've been going out for a few months already, I would like to introduce you to my parents.

Girl: Have you thought about it carefully? Won't it be awkward for you?

Boy: Uh? Why?

Girl: Well... you say your father is a little old-fashioned...

Girl: And I am a girl from the United States, so...

Girl: He might forbid our relationship...

Boy: Whaaat?! You're kidding!

Boy: You are American!? You could have told me so! That's why you were so bad at Japanese when we first met!

Girl: ...

New elements 新しい部首

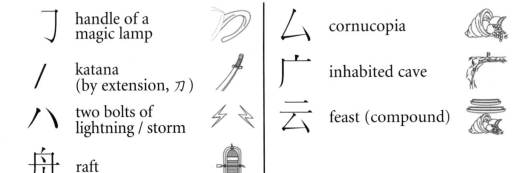

亅	handle of a magic lamp	
丿	katana (by extension, 刀)	
八	two bolts of lightning / storm	
舟	raft	
ム	cornucopia	
广	inhabited cave	
云	feast (compound)	

Lesson 9
第九課

89 (4級)

TEN THOUSAND

マン
- 一万 10,000
- 万年 ten thousand years, an eternity
- 万一 by any chance

バン
- 万歳 Banzai! Hurrah!
- 万国 all nations
- 万能 omnipotent
- 万人 everybody
- 万全 perfection

一 フ 万

(3 strokes)

(注) 方 (90)

(学) This is a magic lamp which multiplies bread: put one slice on it as if it were a lid, and you will get *ten thousand*.

(特) 萬 (old)

---

90 (3級)

PERSON, DIRECTION, SIDE, WAY OF

ホウ
- 四方 the 4 cardinal directions
- 方言 dialect
- 地方 region, area
- 一方 on the other hand

かた
- 方 person (formal)
- 見方 point of view
- 話し方 way of speaking
- 売り方 seller, the selling side

、 一 方 方

(4 strokes)

(注) 万 (89)

(学) A mysterious *person* with a Mexican hat and a magic lamp walks in an unknown *direction*. Radical: 方 .

(特)

91

SWORD, KATANA　（1級）

　(2 strokes)

トウ
名刀 famous sword
日本刀 Japanese katana

かたな
刀 sword
手刀 a karate chop

Special
太刀 long sword
竹刀 bamboo sword

特 釖 (alt)

学 Pictogram of a *katana* resting on a strong arm. It's different from the *exclamation* (26), which always crosses the other element. Radical: 刂, 刀 or 刀.

注 力 (26)

92

CIRCLE, ROUND　（2級）

　(3 strokes)

ガン
弾丸 bullet

まる（い）
丸い circular, round
丸太 log
真ん丸 perfect circle
日の丸 flag of Japan
花丸 Hanamaru
(first name)

特

学 To know how much the now completely *round* belly has grown during the nine months of pregnancy, use a tape measure to measure the *circle* it forms.

注 九 (25)
刃 (8th)

93 (4級) — MINUTE, TO DIVIDE, TO UNDERSTAND

フン

一分 (いっぷん) one minute
二分 (にふん) two minutes
半分 (はんぶん) half
自分 (じぶん) oneself
気分 (きぶん) mood
親分 (おやぶん) boss, chief (mafia)

わ(かる/ける)

分かる (わ) to understand
分ける (わ) to divide amongst, to separate, to sort

ノ 八 分 分

(4 strokes)

注 今 (102)
公 (97)

学 You should *understand* that it takes one *minute* for two bolts of lightning to strike a katana. Radical: 分 .

特

---

94 (3級) — TO CUT, TO DIVIDE

セツ

大切 (たいせつ) important
親切 (しんせつ) kind
切ない (せつ) painful, distressing
切腹 (せっぷく) seppuku

き(る)

切る (き) to cut
裏切る (うらぎ) to betray
切手 (きって) stamp
切符 (きっぷ) ticket
切腹り (はらき) harakiri

一 七 切 切

(4 strokes)

切 切 切 切
切 切 切 切

注 刃 (8th)
初 (4th)

学 This gymnast's exercise *cuts* it really fine, because she uses a sword!

特 切 (alt)

| ` | ハ | ク | 父 |
| 父 | 谷 | 谷 | |

(7 strokes)

VALLEY

谷

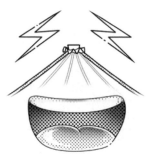

(2級) 95

コク
きょうこく
峡谷 a ravine, gorge

たに
たに
谷 valley
たにがわ
谷川 mountain stream
たにそこ
谷底 bottom of a valley
たにま
谷間 a valley
たにぐち
谷口 Taniguchi (surname)
たにむら
谷村 Tanimura (surname)

  The entrance of the *valley* is also where we place the umbrella that will protect its visitors from the storm (lightning).

合 (101)
容 (5th)

103

`	⼃	⼓	月
月	舟	舟'	舟"
船	船	船	

(11 strokes)

SHIP, BOAT

船

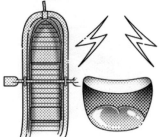

(2級) 96

セン
しょうせん
商船 merchant ship
ふうせん
風船 balloon
せんちょう
船長 ship captain
うちゅうせん
宇宙船 spaceship
せんいん
船員 sailor
きゃくせん
客船 passenger ship

ふね
ふね
船 ship, boat

 船 (alt)
船 (alt)

 When the *ship* sinks, all that is left is a raft with one thirsty survivor who opens his mouth to drink the rainwater when he sees a storm is approaching.

 航 (4th)

97 (2級)

PUBLIC, OFFICIAL

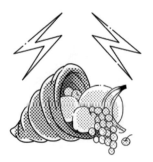

コウ

公正_{こうせい} justice
公園_{こうえん} park
公開_{こうかい} to make public
公衆_{こうしゅう} public
アルバ公_{こう} Duke of Alba
主人公_{しゅじんこう} main character
公文書_{こうぶんしょ} official document

おおやけ

公 (の)_{おおやけ} public, governmental

ノ 八 公 公

(4 strokes)

注 分 (97)
　　会 (100)

学 A cornucopia is a *public* good; it's outdoors even when there's a storm, so that it's at everybody's disposal.

特

---

98 (3級)

BROAD, WIDE

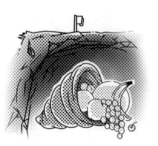

コウ

広告_{こうこく} advertisement
広角_{こうかく} wide-angle (lens)

ひろ (い/まる/める)

広い_{ひろ} wide, large
広場_{ひろば} public square
広島_{ひろしま} Hiroshima
広まる_{ひろ} to spread (eg: a plague)
広める_{ひろ} to propagate (eg: rumors)

丶 亠 广 広
広

(5 strokes)

注 公 (97)
　　庁 (6th)

学 How *wide* must that cave be to hold a never-ending cornucopia.

特 廣 (old)
　　广 (simp)

99

(5 strokes)

PLATFORM, COUNTER FOR MACHINES

(3級)

ダイ
台本 (film) script
台所 kitchen
高台 elevation
灯台 lighthouse

タイ
台北 Taipei (city)
台風 typhoon
舞台 stage

特 臺 (old)
　　坮 (alt)

学 On the ideal *platform* lays a cornucopia feeding the mouth that holds it up.

注 谷 (95)
　 合 (101)
　 古 (103)

100

(6 strokes)

MEETING, ASSOCIATION

(4級)

カイ
会話 conversation
会計 bill
大会 competition
機会 chance
社会 society
会社 company
国会 the Japanese Diet

あ（う）
会う to meet

特 會 (old)

学 A successful *meeting* needs an umbrella for shelter, slices of bread, and lots of food to go with them: a feast under an umbrella.

注 合 (101)
　 今 (102)
　 公 (97)

Exercises 練習

1. Develop the stroke order of the following kanji.

万							
方							
丸							
切							

2. Choose the correct reading for each kanji or kanji combination.

a) それぞれの<u>地方</u>で<u>話し方</u>が違うから、日本語を<u>分かる</u>のは大変ですよ。

Japanese is difficult to understand because every region has a different way of speaking.

地方： 1．ちかた 2．ちがた 3．ちぽう 4．ちほう

話し方： 1．はなしがた 2．はなしかた 3．はなしほう 4．はなしぽう

分かる： 1．うあかる 2．わかる 3．わかかる 4．わる

b) <u>親分</u>に言われたから、<u>日本刀</u>で小指を<u>切って</u>しまったぞ。

Because the boss told me to do so, I cut my pinky finger with the katana.

親分： 1．しんぷん 2．しんぶん 3．おやぶん 4．おやふん

日本刀： 1．にほんと 2．にほんとう 3．にほんち 4．にほんかたな

切って： 1．きって 2．せって 3．せつって 4．きるって

c) フィリアス・フォッグは<u>風船</u>で<u>谷</u>を渡った。

Phileas Fogg crossed the valley on a balloon.

風船： 1．かぜぶね 2．かぜふね 3．かぜせん 4．ふうせん

谷： 1．こく 2．たね 3．たに 4．だに

3. Write the kanji (one or more) and the meaning of the following words.

みかた	_____ _____	きって	_____ _____
たにがわ	_____ _____	こうせい	_____ _____
だいほん	_____ _____	たいかい	_____ _____

4. Correct either the reading or writing mistakes in the following words.

会北	たいぺい	合話	かいわ	公の	おやけの
広園	こうえん	広る	ひろまる	大切	だいせつ

Answers to exercises 練習解答

1. (Check them in the corresponding kanji tables #89, #90, #92, and #94.)

2. a) 地方: 4 │ 話し方: 2 │ 分かる: 2

   b) 親分: 3 │ 日本刀: 2 │ 切って: 1

   c) 風船: 4 │ 谷: 3

3. みかた: 見方, point of view │ きって: 切手, stamp │ たにがわ: 谷川, stream

   こうせい: 公正, justice │ だいほん: 台本, (film) script │ たいかい: 大会, competition

Manga translation マンガ翻訳

Text panel: I am a warrior. Maybe, the best swordsman in the world.

Swordsman: After crossing the wide sea by ship...

Swordsman: Enduring typhoons...

Swordsman: ...And crossing mountains, rivers, and valleys, I've finally... met "that person!"

Swordsman: Hey! Are you the great master who everybody calls "the sword genius?"

Old man: Yes, but wait a minute. Right now, I'm cutting wood.

Swordsman: Be prepared! I have traveled ten thousand kilometers to come and fight with you!

Swordsman (thinking): Uh? Where's my sword?

Swordsman: S-shoot... I left it at home. J-just a minute, I'll be right back, OK?

Swordsman: Oh, and... would you please not tell anybody about this (make this public)?

Old man: ?

New elements 新しい部首

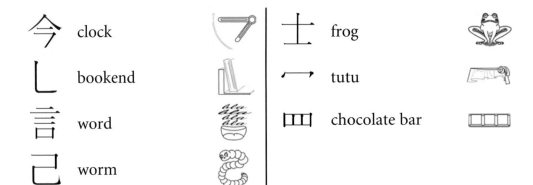

今 clock		士 frog	
∟ bookend		⌐ tutu	
言 word		皿 chocolate bar	
己 worm			

Lesson 10
第十課

101	(3級)	TO FIT, TO AGREE, TO PUT TOGETHER

ゴウ
集合 gathering, meeting
合理 rationality
合意 mutual consent

あ(う)
合う to coincide, to match
話し合う to talk over, to discuss
似合う to suit

ノ	人	合	合
合	合		

(6 strokes)

号	号	**号**	号
号	号	号	**号**

注 会 (100)
谷 (95)
容 (5th)

学 Mouths that *agree* get together to eat bread under an umbrella.

特 閤 (alt)

102	(4級)	NOW

コン
今月 this month
今後 henceforth, from now on

いま
今 now
今時 nowadays

Special
今日 today
今朝 this morning
今年 this year

ノ	人	今	今

(4 strokes)

今	今	**今**	今
今	今	今	**今**

注 合 (101)
会 (100)

学 Pictogram of a clock, with an umbrella for a roof, telling the time to eat bread: *now*.

特 今 (alt)

103 — OLD, ANCIENT (4級)

(5 strokes)

コ
中古 (ちゅうこ) secondhand
古語 (こご) archaic word
古代 (こだい) ancient times
古式 (こしき) ancient ritual

ふる(い)
古い (ふる) old
古本屋 (ふるほんや) secondhand book store
古びる (ふる) to become old
古だぬき (ふる) "old badger" (old grump)

 学 Here you have the *old* custom of kissing the cross with your mouth.

注 苦 (3rd)
舌 (5th)
占 (Jōyō)

---

104 — TO CORRECT, DIRECT, STRAIGHT (2級)

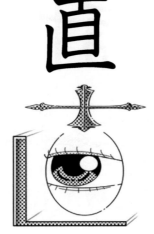

(8 strokes)

チョク
直角 (ちょっかく) right angle
直接 (ちょくせつ) direct
率直 (そっちょく) frank, straightforward

ジキ
正直 (しょうじき) honest

なお(す)
直す (なお) to correct
やり直す (なお) to do over again
書き直す (か なお) to rewrite

 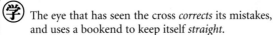 学 The eye that has seen the cross *corrects* its mistakes, and uses a bookend to keep itself *straight*.

注 道 (175)
真 (3rd)

105 (4級)

TO TALK, TO SAY, WORD

ゲン
言語 language
げんご
方言 dialect
ほうげん
提言 proposal
ていげん

い(う)
言う to say
い
言い訳 excuse, explanation
い わけ

こと
言葉 word
こと ば
寝言 to talk in one's sleep
ね ごと

、	二	三	言
言	言	言	

(7 strokes)

注 信 (4th)
舌 (5th)

学 The mouth *talks*, speaking: *words* a mile a minute.
Radical: 訁 or 言.

特 言 (alt)

106 (3級)

TO CALCULATE, TO MEASURE

ケイ
時計 clock, watch
と けい
会計 bill
かいけい
計算 calculation
けいさん
推計 estimate
すいけい
余計 unneeded
よ けい
体温計 thermometer
たいおんけい

はか(る)
計る to calculate,
はか to estimate

、	二	三	言
言	言	言	言
計			

(9 strokes)

注 訂 (Jōyō)
信 (4th)
討 (6th)

学 When you talk next to the cross, you had better *measure* your words.

特

107

丶	二	三	三
言	言	言	言
訁	訐	訏	話
話			

(13 strokes)

話	話	**話**	話
話	话	話	**話**

TO SPEAK, TO TELL

(4級)

ワ
会話 (かいわ) conversation
電話 (でんわ) telephone
世話 (せわ) care, assistance
神話 (しんわ) myth
話題 (わだい) topic

はな (す)
話す (はな) to speak
話し合う (はな・あ) to talk over, to discuss

 特

 学 *Speaking* is the action of one thousand mouths pronouncing words.

 注 語 (108)

108

丶	二	三	三
訁	言	言	言
訁	訝	語	語
語	語		

(14 strokes)

語	語	**語**	語
語	语	語	**語**

LANGUAGE, TO TELL TO RELATE

(4級)

ゴ
言語 (げんご) language
国語 (こくご) national language
外国語 (がいこくご) foreign language
日本語 (にほんご) Japanese
フランス語 (ご) French
落語 (らくご) comical storytelling

かた (る)
語る (かた) to tell, to relate
物語 (ものがたり) tale, story

 特

 学 Words pronounced by mouths in the five continents are, of course, in different *languages*.

 注 話 (107)

109　(2級)

HISTORY, CHRONICLE, TO WRITE DOWN

キ
記者 journalist, reporter
記事 article, story
記入 entry, to fill in
日記 diary
伝記 biography
記録 record
暗記する to memorize
書記 secretary

記

(10 strokes)

注 訳 (6°)
　妃 (4°)

学 The worm has a diary where she *writes down* her words.

特

110　(3級)

TO SELL

バイ
売店 stand, stall
売買 trade
売春 prostitution
商売 business, transaction
売買品 product for sale

う(る)
売る to sell
売り出す to put on sale

売

(7 strokes)

注 読 (114)
　壱 (Jōyō)
　受 (3rd)

学 The frog wears a tutu exposing her slender legs in order to *sell* more.

特 賣 (old)

111

TO BUY

(4級)

(12 strokes)

バイ
買収 to buy, to purchase
売買 trade

か(う)
買う to buy
買物 shopping
買い手 buyer
買い得 bargain
買い取り purchase

(特)

(学) You look at the chocolate bar with an eye as big as a saucer, shake your legs and run to *buy* it!

(注) 貢 (Jōyō)
貫 (Jōyō)
貰 (not Jōyō)

112

VOICE

(3級)

(7 strokes)

セイ
音声 sound, voice
声帯 vocal cords
名声 fame

こえ
声 voice
大声 loud voice
小声 whisper
叫び声 scream

(特) 聲 (old)

(学) The frog loves a good *voice*: that is why she uses opera glasses when she goes to the opera.

(注) 斉 (Jōyō)

川田（かわだ）く〜ん‼

川田（かわだ）くん、古だぬきの部長（ぶちょう）が君（きみ）と話し合（あ）いたがっていますよ。

わ…分（わ）かった。彼（かれ）の声（こえ）を聞（き）いたよ！

この間（あいだ）のキャンペーンは大失敗（だいしっぱい）だ！早（はや）くやり直（なお）さなければ、倒産（とうさん）だぞ‼やっぱり、この仕事（しごと）はベテランに任（まか）せたほうがよかった！

でも、部長（ぶちょう）…この新（あたら）しい「コンピューター携帯（けいたい）」はすばらしい製品（せいひん）です。今（いま）からだんだん売（う）られていくようになると思（おも）います…

だらだらを言（い）うな！この記録（きろく）を見（み）ろ！売（う）り上（あ）げの推計（すいけい）だ。誰（だれ）も買（か）ってないよ‼

確（たし）かに、その携帯（けいたい）はいいものだけど…バッテリーが大（おお）きくて余計（よけい）で不便（ふべん）だ！何語（なにご）で言（い）えば分（わ）かるんだ、バカ者（もの）‼?

グ〜ン

Exercises 練習

1. Develop the stroke order of the following kanji.

語									
記									
売									
声									

2. Choose the correct reading for each kanji or kanji combination.

a) 売店のおばさんは声がでかい。

The woman at the stall yells a lot.

売店： 1．ばいてん 2．うみせ 3．うて 4．はいてん

声： 1．ごえ 2．こえ 3．こうえ 4．せい

b) この計算は正しくないよ。早くやり直しなさい！

This calculation is not correct. Do it over again, quickly!

計算 1．はかさん 2．はさん 3．けさん 4．けいさん

やり直し：1．やりちょくし 2．やりじきし 3．やりなし 4．やりなおし

c) 今月、日本の古代の神話の本が出る。楽しみ！

This month, a book on myths in ancient times comes out.

今月： 1．こんがつ 2．こがつ 3．こげつ 4．こんげつ

古代： 1．ごだい 2．こだい 3．ふだい 4．ふるだい

神話： 1．しんば 2．しんわ 3．しんばなし 4．かみばなし

3. Write the kanji (one or more) and the meaning of the following words.

はなしあう ＿＿＿＿ ＿＿＿＿ ちゅうこ ＿＿＿＿ ＿＿＿＿

しょうじき ＿＿＿＿ ＿＿＿＿ ほうげん ＿＿＿＿ ＿＿＿＿

かいけい ＿＿＿＿ ＿＿＿＿ かいて ＿＿＿＿ ＿＿＿＿

4. Correct either the reading or writing mistakes in the following words.

言い訳	いわけ	合意	あいい	今朝	こんあさ
古本屋	こほんや	真接	ちょくせつ	語言	げんご
物語	ものご	読春	ばいしゅん	言者	きしゃ

Answers to exercises 練習解答

1. (Check them in the corresponding kanji tables #108, #109, #110, and #112)

2. a) 売店 : 1 | 声 : 2 // b) 計算 : 4 | やり直し : 4 // c) 今月 : 4 | 古代 : 2 | しんわ : 2

3. はなしあう : 話し合う, to talk over, to discuss | ちゅうこ : 中古, secondhand

しょうじき : 正直, honest | ほうげん : 方言, dialect | かいけい : 会計, bill

かいて : 買い手, buyer

4. 言い訳 いいわけ | 合意 ごうい | 今朝 けさ | 古本屋 ふるほんや | 直接 ちょくせつ

言語 げんご | 物語 ものがたり | 売春 ばいしゅん | 記者 きしゃ

Manga translation マンガ翻訳

Voice: Kawadaaa!!

Colleague: Kawada, I think that grumpy boss wants to talk to you.

Kawada: Yes, I heard him!

Boss: This last campaign is a total failure! If we don't do it over again, we will go bankrupt! Oh, I should have entrusted a veteran with this job!

Kawada: But, boss... The new "computer-mobile" is an excellent product. I think it will sell more and more.

Boss: Don't give me any of your stories! Look at the records: these are sale estimates. Nobody is going to buy it!

Boss: Indeed, that mobile is a wonder... But the battery is big, useless, and uncomfortable! In what language do you want me to say it?! You fool!

Onomatopoeia: Goooof

New elements 新しい部首

聿 colored pencils	厂 cliff
氏 scroll	且 ladder
泉 fountain	寺 Buddhist temple

Lesson 11
第十一課

113 (4級) TO WRITE

ショ

書道 calligraphy
文書 text, sentence
証明書 certificate, diploma

か(く)

書く to write
書き順 (kanji) stroke order
下書き rough draft
後書き epilogue

（注）筆 (3rd)
春 (156)
曹 (Jōyō)

ㄱ ㄱ ㄱ 聿
亖 聿 聿 書
書 書

(10 strokes)

書 書 **書** 書
書 書 壽 **書**

（学）*Write* with colored pencils, in the sunshine.

（特）書 (alt)

120

114 (4級) TO READ

ドク

読者 reader
読書 to read, reading
読書室 reading room

よ(む)

読む to read
音読み *on'yomi* kanji reading
立読み to read while standing (for free, in a book store)

` ニ ㇐ 言
言 言 言 言
計 計 計 訪
詩 読

(14 strokes)

読 読 **読** 読
読 読 読 **読**

（注）売 (110)
設 (5th)

（学）There is nothing that this frog with a tutu and slender legs likes best than *reading* beautiful words.

（特）讀 (old)

115

LIGHT, RAY (3級)

光

(6 strokes)

コウ
日光 にっこう sunlight; Nikkō city
月光 げっこう moonlight
光栄 こうえい honor
観光 かんこう tourism

ひかり
光 ひかり light
光物 ひかりもの luminous body

ひか（る）
光る ひか to shine, to be bright

 炎 (alt)
茨 (alt)

 The dwarf has seen the *light*: the one emitted by this tempting bread slice and slender legs.

 元 (116)
先 (41)

116

ORIGIN, FORMER (3級)

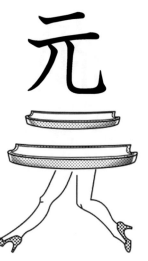

元

(4 strokes)

ゲン
元気 げんき vigor, energy
元価 げんか cost price
十元 じゅうげん 10 yuan
(Chinese currency)

ガン
元祖 がんそ the founder

もと
元 もと origin, cause
事故の元 じこ もと cause of an accident

 Temptation, personified by these slices of bread and slender legs, is the *origin* of everything in this world.

 光 (115)
先 (41)
兄 (215)

117 (2級)

DRAWING, PICTURE

絵

カイ

絵画 <ruby>絵<rt>かい</rt></ruby><ruby>画<rt>が</rt></ruby> picture, work of art

え

絵 <ruby>絵<rt>え</rt></ruby> drawing, picture
絵本 <ruby>絵<rt>え</rt></ruby><ruby>本<rt>ほん</rt></ruby> picture book
絵描き <ruby>絵<rt>え</rt></ruby><ruby>描<rt>か</rt></ruby>き painter, artist
油絵 <ruby>油<rt>あぶら</rt></ruby><ruby>絵<rt>え</rt></ruby> oil painting
絵馬 <ruby>絵<rt>え</rt></ruby><ruby>馬<rt>ま</rt></ruby> *ema* votive tablet
絵葉書 <ruby>絵<rt>え</rt></ruby><ruby>葉<rt>は</rt></ruby><ruby>書<rt>がき</rt></ruby> postcard

く 乡 纟 糸
糸 糸 糽 給
給 絵 絵 絵

(12 strokes)

絵 絵 **絵** 絵
絵 絵 絵 **絵**

注 給 (4th)

紛 (Jōyō)

学 For an open-air *picture* exhibition we will need the following items: thread to hang the pictures, an umbrella in case it rains, and a feast for when we are hungry.

特 繪 (old)

118 (3級)

PAPER

紙

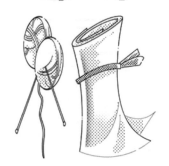

シ

和紙 <ruby>和<rt>わ</rt></ruby><ruby>紙<rt>し</rt></ruby> Japanese paper
白紙 <ruby>白<rt>はく</rt></ruby><ruby>紙<rt>し</rt></ruby> blank sheet of paper
用紙 <ruby>用<rt>よう</rt></ruby><ruby>紙<rt>し</rt></ruby> form (to be filled out)
紙上 <ruby>紙<rt>し</rt></ruby><ruby>上<rt>じょう</rt></ruby> on paper
表紙 <ruby>表<rt>ひょう</rt></ruby><ruby>紙<rt>し</rt></ruby> cover, binding

かみ

紙 <ruby>紙<rt>かみ</rt></ruby> paper
紙切れ <ruby>紙<rt>かみ</rt></ruby><ruby>切<rt>き</rt></ruby>れ scrap of paper
手紙 <ruby>手<rt>て</rt></ruby><ruby>紙<rt>がみ</rt></ruby> letter

く 乡 纟 糸
糸 糸 紅 紅
紙 紙

(10 strokes)

紙 紙 **紙** 紙
紙 紙 紙 **紙**

注 組 (121)

級 (3rd)

学 Pictogram of the most ancient form of *paper*: the scroll with (on the left) the thread to bind it.

特 帋 (alt)

LINE

（2級）

(15 strokes)

線

セン

ちょくせん
直線 straight line
かせん
下線 underlined
こうせん
光線 light beam
いちばんせん
一番線 track #1
　　　　(train or subway)
でんせん
電線 telephone line
かいせん
回線 circuit
しゃみせん
三味線 shamisen (three-
　　　　stringed guitar)
ちへいせん
地平線 horizon

特 綫 (alt)

学 Thread is the extremely fine *line* that separates the fountain of life from death.

注 泉 (6th)
綿 (5th)
緒 (Jōyō)

FIELD, PLAIN, ORIGIN

（2級）

(10 strokes)

原

ゲン

げんや
原野 wilderness, plain
そうげん
草原 grassland
げんいん
原因 cause
げんさく
原作 original work
げんし
原子 atom
げんこう
原稿 manuscript

はら

はら
原 plain, field
のはら
野原 Nohara (surname)

特 原 (alt)
原 (alt)

学 Under the white midday sun, at the foot of a cliff, the dwarf runs around the *plain*.

注 泉 (6th)
源 (6th)
厚 (5th)

121 (2級) TEAM, GROUP

ソ
組織 organization (そしき)
組成 component (そせい)

くみ
組 team, group (くみ)
番組 (radio or TV) program (ばんぐみ)
組合わせる to combine (くみあ)
仕組 plan, plot (しくみ)
組合 association, union (くみあい)
組長 mafia boss (くみちょう)

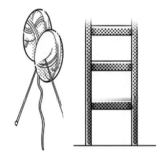

(11 strokes)

注 紺 (Jōyō)
　　紙 (118)

学 Here is the thread that unites the neighbors with the same ladder: the residents *association*.

特

---

122 (2級) THIN, DETAIL

サイ
細工 workmanship (さいく)
明細 details, particulars (めいさい)

ほそ(い)
細い thin, fine, narrow (ほそ)
細長い long and thin (ほそなが)
心細い forlorn, disheartened (こころぼそ)

こま(かい)
細かい detailed, meticulous (こま)

(11 strokes)

注 組 (121)
　　紳 (Jōyō)
　　紬 (Jōyō)

学 Visualize the irrigation ditch, the *fine* thread of water that keeps the rice field humid.

特

124

123

BUDDHIST TEMPLE (2級)

(6 strokes)

ジ
古寺 (こじ) old temple
金閣寺 (きんかくじ) Kinkakuji (temple in Kyoto)

てら
お寺 (てら) temple
山寺 (やまでら) mountain temple
寺参り (てらまいり) to go to a temple to worship
清水寺 (きよみずでら) Kiyomizudera (temple in Kyoto)

特

学 Pictogram of a *Buddhist temple*. Its origin is a Buddhist alien watering the fertile land.

注 持 (3rd)
待 (3rd)
去 (3rd)

124

HOUR, TIME (4級)

(10 strokes)

ジ
時間 (じかん) hour, time
何時 (なんじ)？ What's the time?
時代 (じだい) age, era
時事 (じじ) current events
時季 (じき) season

とき
あの時 (とき) that time
時時 (ときどき) sometimes

Special
時計 (とけい) clock, watch

特 旹 (alt)

学 The position of the sun indicates the passing of *time*: there is no better way to know the time at a Buddhist temple.

注 寺 (123)
持 (3rd)
待 (3rd)

この物語は無人の寺で始まります。

年を取った研究者が古い原稿を見つけた時…

その本の表紙に書かれていた変な絵に気が付かず…

ある呪文を読み始めると、天井からまぶしくて細い光線が落ちてきました！

その呪文と光線の組み合わせで出た効果は…「スーパーオジイサン」の元でした!!

が、スーパーオジイサンの唯一のスーパーパワーは六時間のスーパー昼寝をできるぐらいです…がんばれ、スーパーオジイサン!! 正義と平和を守って!!

Exercises 練習

1. Develop the stroke order of the following kanji.

書								
紙								
細								
寺								

2. Choose the correct reading for each kanji or kanji combination.

a) 書き順、訓読み、音読みまで覚えなければならない。もう漢字はいやだ！

We must remember stroke order, kun'yomi, *and even* on'yomi. *I'm fed up with kanji!*

書き順： 1．かききじゅん 2．かきじゅん 3．しょじゅん 4．しょきじゅん

音読み： 1．ねよみ 2．ねどく 3．おんよみ 4．おんどく

b) 時間が遅れていたから、スピードを出しすぎました。それは事故の元です。

Because it was getting late, he went too fast. That was the cause of the accident.

時間 1．じかん 2．しかん 3．ときあいだ 4．ときどき

元： 1．げん 2．けん 3．がん 4．もと

c) 清水寺を訪ねた時、三味線を弾いている女性がいました。

When I visited Kiyomizudera, there was a woman playing the shamisen.

清水寺： 1．きよみずてら 2．きよみすてら 3．きよみずでら 4．きよみすでら

時： 1．じ 2．し 3．とき 4．どき

三味線： 1．さんみぜん 2．さんみせん 3．しゃみせん 4．しゃみぜん

3. Write the kanji (one or more) and the meaning of the following words.

したがき ＿＿＿＿＿ ＿＿＿＿＿   どくしょ ＿＿＿＿＿ ＿＿＿＿＿

えはがき ＿葉＿ ＿＿＿＿＿   かみきれ ＿＿＿＿＿ ＿＿＿＿＿

ちょくせん ＿＿＿＿＿ ＿＿＿＿＿   くみあい ＿＿＿＿＿ ＿＿＿＿＿

4. Correct either the reading or writing mistakes in the following words.

観光	かんこ	売者	どくしゃ	会本	えほん
絵画	えが	泉因	げんいん	金閣時	きんかくじ
持代	じだい	細い	こまかい	番組	ばんくみ

Answers to exercises　練習解答

1. (Check them in the corresponding kanji tables #113, #118, #122, and #123.)

2. a) 書き順: 2 | 音読み: 3 // b) 時間: 1 | 元: 4 // c) 清水寺: 3 | 時: 3 | 三味線: 3

3. したがき: 下書き, rough draft | どくしょ: 読書, to read, reading | えはがき: 絵葉書, postcard | かみきれ: 紙切れ, scrap of paper | ちょくせん: 直線, straight line | くみあい: 組合, association, union

4. 観光 かんこう | 読者 どくしゃ | 絵本 えほん | 絵画 かいが | 原因 げんいん

　　金閣寺 きんかくじ | 時代 じだい | 細かい こまかい or 細い ほそい | 番組 ばんぐみ

Manga translation　マンガ翻訳

Text panel: Our story starts in an abandoned temple.

Text panel: When an old investigator found an ancient manuscript...

Text panel: He didn't notice the strange drawing it had on the cover...

Text panel: When he started reading a certain spell, a fine and blinding beam of light descended from the ceiling!

Text panel: The combined effect of the spell and the beam was the origin of the... Super Grandfather!

Text panel: Still, the Super Grandfather's only superpower is taking Super six-hour Naps... Go on, Super Grandfather! Defend peace and justice!

New elements　新しい部首

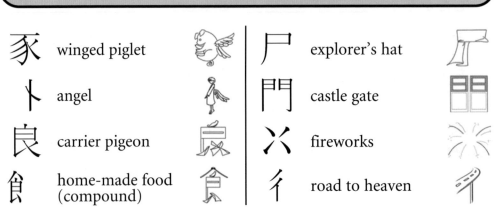

豕　winged piglet

⺊　angel

良　carrier pigeon

food　home-made food (compound)

尸　explorer's hat

門　castle gate

㐅　fireworks

彳　road to heaven

Lesson　12
第十二課

125 (3級)

HOUSE, FAMILY

カ / ケ

家族 (かぞく) family
家計 (かけい) family finances
家内 (かない) wife
作家 (さっか) author, writer
川口家 (かわぐちけ) Kawaguchi family

いえ / うち / や

家出 (いえで) to run away from home
家 (うち) or 家 (いえ) home, house
家賃 (やちん) house rent

(10 strokes)

(注) 豚 (Jōyō)
案 (4th)
実 (3rd)

(学) This little piglet with wings is the cousin of "The three little pigs," and his family is hiding him under the roof of a *house*.

(特)

---

126 (3級)

ROOM, CHAMBER

シツ

和室 (わしつ) Japanese-style room
洋室 (ようしつ) Western-style room
教室 (きょうしつ) classroom
室内 (しつない) indoors
寝室 (しんしつ) bedroom

むろ

室町 (むろまち) Muromachi (suburb in Kyoto)
小室 (こむろ) Komuro (surname)

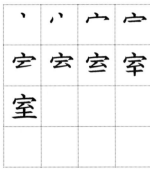

(9 strokes)

(注) 至 (6th)
害 (4th)

(学) Your favorite *room*: under the cover of a roof, with never-ending bread and food, because there is still fertile land.

(特)

127

INSIDE, BELONGING (2級)

(4 strokes)

ナイ
内科 *ないか* internal medicine
国内 *こくない* national
家内 *かない* wife
内緒 *ないしょ* secret

うち
内 *うち* inside, within
内の人 *うち ひと* someone inside (family, company)
(若い)内に *わか うち* while (you're young)

特 内 (alt)

学 Be careful with Kim: you may wear a wig, but he'll get *inside* your head.

注 肉 (129)
丙 (Jōyō)

128

OUTSIDE, OUTDOORS, TO REMOVE (4級)

(5 strokes)

ガイ
外見 *がいけん* external appearance
外出 *がいしゅつ* outing, excursion
外国人 *がいこくじん* foreigner
海外 *かいがい* overseas

そと
外 *そと* outside, outdoors
外村 *そとむら* Sotomura (surname)

はず(す)
外す *はず* to remove

特

学 The angel pushes the moon *outside*: it has to leave, because night is ending.

注 多 (85)
名 (46)

129 (3級)

MEAT

ニク
- 肉 meat (にく)
- 肉まん meat bun (にく)
- 牛肉 beef (ぎゅうにく)
- 豚肉 pork (ぶたにく)
- 筋肉 muscle (きんにく)
- 肉体 the body / flesh (にくたい)
- 肉親 blood relative (にくしん)
- 肉欲 carnal desire (にくよく)

(6 strokes)

注 内 (127)

学 When Kim gets inside your head twice, it can only mean one thing: he's hungry for *meat*...

特 肉 (alt)
宍 (alt)

130 (4級)

TO EAT

ショク
- 和食 Japanese food (わしょく)
- 夕食 dinner (ゆうしょく)
- 外食 to eat out (がいしょく)
- 食後 after a meal (しょくご)

た(べる)
- 食べる to eat (た)
- 食べ物 food (た)(もの)

く(う)
- 食う to eat (colloquial) (く)

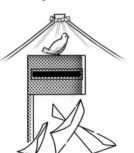

(9 strokes)

注 良 (4th)
倉 (4th)

学 This evokes home, and eating home-made *food*: the pigeon resting on the mailbox, under the umbrella. Can't you just smell mommy's soup? Radical: 食 .

特 食 (alt)
喰 (hom)

131 （2級）

DOOR

(4 strokes)

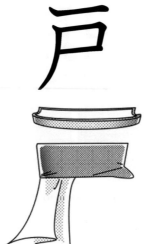

コ
- こ別 from door to door
- こ外 outdoor, open-air
- こ籍 family register

と
- と戸 door
- 井戸 (water) well
- 戸口 doorway

Special
- こうべ神戸 Kōbe (city)

 戸 (alt)

学 An explorer never arrives empty-handed: just take a look at the slice of bread he brings when he crosses the *door*.

注 声 (112)
尺 (6th)

133

---

132 （3級）

GATE, FRONT DOOR

(8 strokes)

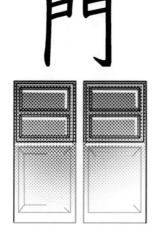

モン
- こうもん校門 school gate
- せいもん正門 front gate
- にゅうもん入門 introduction
- めいもん名門 famous family
- せんもんか専門家 specialist
- もんばん門番 gatekeeper
- もんげん門限 curfew

かど
- かどちが お門違い the wrong place

 门 (simp)

学 Pictogram of the *gate* of a castle.

注 問 (3rd)
間 (133)
聞 (134)

133 (4級)

SPACE, INTERVAL

間

カン / ゲン

空間 (an open) space
くうかん

時間 time, hour
じかん

人間 person, human being
にんげん

世間 world, society
せけん

ま

昼間 daytime
ひるま

間に合う to be in time for
ま　あ

あいだ

長い間 a long time
なが　あいだ

丨 冂 冂 冂
冂 門 門 門
門 門 間 間

(12 strokes)

間 間 **間** 间
間 闁 間 **間**

注 門 (132)
　 問 (3rd)
　 聞 (134)

学 Notice the time *interval* from the moment the sun rises until it is over the castle gate.

特 閒 (alt)

---

134 (4級)

TO HEAR, TO LISTEN, TO ASK

聞

ブン

新聞 newspaper
しんぶん

風聞 rumor
ふうぶん

き (く / こえる)

聞く to listen
き

聞き取り listening
き　と　(comprehension)

聞き忘れる to forget
き　わす　what one hears

(海が) 聞こえる
うみ　(the sea) can be heard

丨 冂 冂 冂
冂 門 門 門
門 門 門 間
間 聞

(14 strokes)

聞 聞 **聞** 闻
聞 闻 聞 **聞**

注 門 (132)
　 問 (3rd)
　 間 (133)

学 If you hold your ear close to the castle gate, you'll *hear* what's brewing inside.

特

(7 strokes)

TO COME

(4級)

ライ
らいにち
来日 to come to Japan
らいねん
来年 next year
みらい
未来 future
せいらい
生来 by nature
ほんらい
本来 originally

く(る)
く
来る to come
あさ　く
(朝が)来る
(the morning) comes

特 來 (old)
　徠 (alt)
　耒 (alt)

学 You must *come*! There will be a religious service and fireworks before and after the bread. Don't miss it!

注 乗 (3rd)
　米 (81)
　末 (4th)

(6 strokes)

**TO GO, LINE,
TO CARRY OUT**

(4級)

コウ
じっこう
実行 to put into practice
りょこう
旅行 trip
こうどう
行動 action, behavior
たんこうぼん
単行本 separate volume

ギョウ
に ぎょう め
二行目 second line

い(く)/おこな(う)
い
行く to go
おこな
行う to carry out, to do

特

学 Pictogram of a highway that seems to be *going* towards the sky, and of another horizontal, more worldly one. The left part (彳) works as an element of other kanji.

注

いいお天気だね！公園で肉まんなんか食べにいこうかな…

そう言えば…この間、パンツを盗むのに女の子を襲う人が出るという噂を聞いた…

あら！門のそばに怪しいやつがいる！

とりあえず、外に出かけることを諦めるわ。

ハッハッハ逃げ場がないぞ！残念だな、僕のほしい宝物は君が持っているぜ！オレのものだ!!

あっ！あ…あの音…まさか！家に入ったのか!?

キャアー!!知らない内に、寝室の戸口まで来てる!!来るな!!

ガチャー

僕、専門家じゃないけど、金貨みたいだね。ん？姉ちゃん？どうしたの？

姉ちゃん！見て、見て！この貯金箱の中にめずらしいコインがあったぞ！

Exercises　練習

1. Develop the stroke order of the following kanji.

家									
食									
来									
行									

2. Choose the correct reading for each kanji or kanji combination.

a) 神戸は外国人が多い町だから、色々_{いろいろ}なところの食べ物を食べられるよ。

Kobe is a city with many foreigners, so you can eat food from various places.

神戸：　1．こべ　　　　2．こおべ　　　　3．こべえ　　　　4．こうべ

外国人：1．はっこくじん 2．はずこくじん 3．がいこくじん 4．そとこくじん

食べ物：1．くべもの　　2．たべもの　　　3．くいべもの　4．しょくべもの

b) 家には門限というのはないけど、夜遅_{おそ}くなるとお父_{とう}さん怖_{こわ}いよ！

At home, there is no curfew at night, but if it gets late, my father can be scary!

家：　　1．いいえ　　2．や　　　　3．うち　　　　4．か

門限：　1．もげん　　2．かげん　　3．もんげん　　4．かんげん

c) 外へ行きたかったから、赤_{あか}ちゃんはベルトを外して、車を出ちゃった。

Because he wanted to go outside, the baby removed his seat belt, and got out of the car.

外：　　1．がい　　　2．はず　　　3．はずす　　4．そと

行き：　1．おき　　　2．おこなき　3．いき　　　4．いくき

外して：1．はずずして　2．はずして　　3．はすして　　4．そとして

3. Write the kanji (one or more) and the meaning of the following words.

いえで　　　_____ _____　　きょうしつ _____ _____

かない　　　_____ _____　　がいしゅつ _____ _____

ゆうしょく _____ _____　　こうもん　　_____ _____

4. Correct either the reading or writing mistakes in the following words.

空間	くかん	人門	にんげん	内まん	きんにくまん
新問	しんぶん	旅行	りょうこ	本未	ほんらい

Answers to exercises 練習解答

1. (Check them in the corresponding kanji tables #125, #130, #135, and #136)

2. a) 神戸: 4 | 外国人: 3 | 食べ物: 2 // b) 家: 3 | 門限: 3 // c) 外: 4 | 行き: 3 | 外して: 2

3. いえで: 家出, to run away from home | きょうしつ: 教室, classroom

かない: 家内, wife | がいしゅつ: 外出, excursion

ゆうしょく: 夕食, dinner | こうもん: 校門, school gate

4. 空間 くうかん | 人間 にんげん | 肉まん にくまん

新聞 しんぶん | 旅行 りょ~こう | 本来 ほんらい

Manga translation マンガ翻訳

Girl: What a beautiful day! I could go to the park to eat a meat bun, for example...

Girl (thinking): Oh, there's a very suspicious man by the gate.

Girl (thinking): Now that I think of it... Lately, I've heard some rumors about a bad guy who attacks girls to steal their panties...

Man (in the scene in her imagination): Ha, ha ha ha

Girl (imagines): Waaah!

Girl (thinking): For the moment, I had better forget about going out.

Noise: Boom

Girl: Oh! T...that noise... Don't tell me! Has he got into my house?!

Voice: Ha, ha, ha! You have no way out!

Voice: I'm sorry, but you have a treasure I want for me... And it will be mine!!

Sound of the door: Squeak

Girl: Aaah, he's come as far as my bedroom! Nooo, don't come near me!

Younger brother: Sister! Look, look! Inside this moneybox there was a very strange coin! I'm not a specialist on this subject, but it looks like a gold coin, doesn't it?

Younger brother: Uh? Sister? What's wrong?

New elements 新しい部首

寸 scarecrow

午 slide with steps

羽 wings

隹 swan

午 suit hanger with hat

夂 swimmer

Lesson　13
第十三課

137 (2級)

TALENT, AGE

サイ

てんさい
天才 genius
さいじん
才人 talented person
さいのう
才能 talent
てんさいじ
天才児 child prodigy
あくさい
悪才 evil genius
さんさい
(三)才 (three) years old
ごがく　さい
(語学)の才 talent, ability
(for languages)

一 十 才

(3 strokes)

注 木 (59)

才 (Kana)

学 Pictogram of a scarecrow with a commemorative band rewarding his *talent*.

特 纔 (old)

---

138 (3級)

FACTORY, CONSTRUCTION

コウ

こうがく
工学 engineering
こうじょう
工場 factory
こうぎょう
工業 industry
こうじ
工事 building work, construction
こうさく
工作 construction

ク

だいく
大工 carpenter
くふう
工夫 invention, device

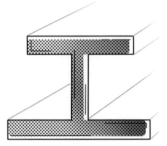

一 丁 工

(3 strokes)

注 王 (15)

工 (Kana)

学 Pictogram of an iron beam, a key piece in *construction*. Radical: 工 .

特 丂 (alt)

139

TO MAKE, TO ELABORATE

(3級)

(7 strokes)

サク
作家 author, writer
作文 composition
新作 new work
工作 construction

つく（る）
作る to make
作り話 made-up story

特 做(old)
造(hom)
創(hom)

学 Kim presents the newest article he has *made*: the slide.

注 竹 (71)
伊 (Jōyō)

140

FEATHER, WING

(2級)

(6 strokes)

ハ
羽音 flapping of wings

ワ
一羽 one bird
五羽 five birds

はね
羽 wing
矢羽 arrow feathers
羽田 Haneda (place name)

特 羽 (alt)

学 Pictogram of two *wings*.
Radical: 羽 , 羽 or 羽.

注 竹 (71)
飛 (4th)

141 (3級)

ヨウ

曜日 day of the week
<ruby>よう<rt>よう</rt></ruby>び

月曜日 Monday
<ruby>げつ<rt>げつ</rt></ruby>よう び

火曜日 Tuesday
か よう び

水曜日 Wednesday
すい よう び

木曜日 Thursday
もく よう び

金曜日 Friday
きん よう び

土曜日 Saturday
ど よう び

日曜日 Sunday
にち よう び

DAY OF THE WEEK

日	日	日	日
日	日	日	日
日	日	日	日
曜	曜	曜	

(18 strokes)

曜	曜	**曜**	曜
曜	曜	曜	**曜**

注 濯 (Jōyō)
　　 耀 (Jōyō)

学 Here is a picture of a swan, spreading its wings as the sun rises in the morning, every *day of the week*.

特 曜 (alt)
　　 旺 (alt)

---

142 (3級)

チョウ

朝食 breakfast
ちょう しょく

北朝鮮 North Korea
きた ちょう せん

あさ

朝市 morning market
あさ いち

毎朝 every morning
まい あさ

朝日 Asahi (brand)
あさ ひ

Especial

今朝 this morning
け さ

MORNING

一	十	十	古
古	古	直	卓
朝	朝	朝	朝

(12 strokes)

朝	朝	**朝**	朝
朝	朝	朝	**朝**

注 湖 (3rd)

　　 幹 (5th)
　　 潮 (6th)

学 *Mornings* are for devotees of the cross, who get up early when the sun rises and the moon leaves.

特

143

(9 strokes)

DAYTIME, NOON

(3級)

チュウ
昼食 (ちゅうしょく) lunch
昼光 (ちゅうこう) daylight

ひる
昼 (ひる) noon
昼ご飯 (ひる・はん) lunch
昼寝 (ひる・ね) nap
昼も夜も (ひる・よる) day and night

 晝 (alt)

 During the *daytime*, the explorer walks relentlessly in the sun, and only stops to eat his slice of bread.

注 間 (133)
宣 (6th)

143

144

(13 strokes)

EASY, FUN, MUSIC

(3級)

ガク
音楽 (おんがく) music
楽屋 (がく・や) dressing room

ラク
楽 (らく) easy, simple
楽天家 (らくてん・か) optimist
楽園 (らく・えん) Paradise

たの(しい)
楽しい (たの) fun
楽しみ (たの) hope, expectation

特 樂 (alt)

 A white sun with phenomenal eyes has *fun* with the *musical* show of fireworks over a tree.

注 薬 (3rd)
集 (3rd)

145 (4級)

MIDDAY

ゴ
 正午 midday
午前 morning
午後 afternoon

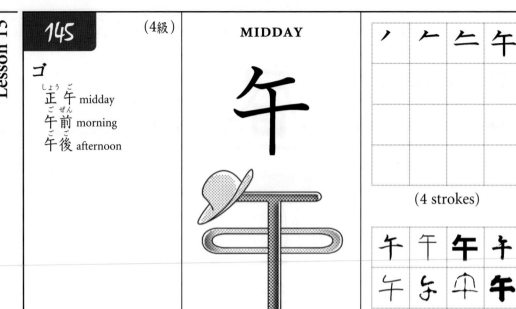

ノ ┌ 二 午

(4 strokes)

注 牛 (146)
平 (3rd)
干 (6th)

学 At *midday*, the bald man hangs his hat on the suit hanger, so his bald head gets some sun.

特

---

146 (3級)

COW, BULL, OX

ギュウ
牛肉 beef, veal
牛丼 bowl of rice with beef
牛車 oxcart
牛乳 milk
野牛 buffalo

うし
牛 cow, ox
子牛 calf

牛

ノ ┌ 二 牛

(4 strokes)

注 午 (145)
年 (40)

学 Full pictogram of a squashed *cow*, which appeared already in number 41.
Radical: 牛 .

特

147

STAR, PLANET (2級)

(9 strokes)

セイ
火星（か せい） Mars
金星（きん せい） Venus
惑星（わく せい） planet
星座（せい ざ） constellation

ほし
星（ほし） star, planet
星空（ほし ぞら） starry sky
星明（ほし あ）り starlight
星占（ほし うらな）い astrology

 皇 (alt)

 The sun is the *star* that gives us life.

 皇 (6th)
臭 (Jōyō)

148

NIGHT (3級)

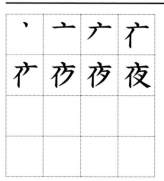

(8 strokes)

ヤ
今夜（こん や） tonight
深夜（しん や） wee hours of the night
夜会（や かい） evening party
夜学（や がく） night school

ヨ
夜明（よ あ）け dawn
夜中（よ なか） midnight

よる
夜（よる） night

 Kim experiences a Mexican *night* while his friend, who hopes to be a swimmer, trains in the waters of the Pacific.

 死 (3rd)
液 (5th)

Exercises 練習

1. Develop the stroke order of the following kanji.

曜								
朝								
楽								
夜								

2. Choose the correct reading for each kanji or kanji combination.

a) 原作はできていなかったので、深夜まで働^{はたら}くことにした。

Since I had not finished the book, I decided to work until the wee hours of the night.

原作： 1．げんつく　　　2．げんさく　　3．はらつくり　4．はらつく

深夜： 1．しんよ　　　　2．しんや　　　3．しんよる　　4．しんやる

b) 娘^{むすめ}は音楽の天才です。今度^{こんど}のコンサートで新作を発表^{はっぴょう}する予定^{よてい}です。

My daughter is a genius for music. In the next concert, she will present her new work.

音楽：　1．おんらく　2．ねらく　　　3．おんがく　　4．ねがく

天才：　1．てんさい　2．てんざい　　3．あまさい　　4．あまざい

新作：　1．しんつく　2．しんじゅく　3．しんさく　　4．しんざく

c) 工事が遅^{おく}れているから、日曜日を含^{ふく}めて毎日頑張^{まいにちがんば}りましょう。

Since we are behind schedule in the construction,

we are going to work every day, Sundays included.

工事：　1．こじ　　　2．ごじ　　　3．こうじ　　　4．くじ

日曜日： 1．にちよび　2．ひよび　　3．にちよび　　4．にちようび

3. Write the kanji (one or more) and the meaning of the following words.

つくりばなし ＿＿＿ ＿＿＿　　かようび　　＿＿＿ ＿＿＿

あさひ　　　 ＿＿＿ ＿＿＿　　かせい　　　＿＿＿ ＿＿＿

ぎゅうにく　 ＿＿＿ ＿＿＿　　やがく　　　＿＿＿ ＿＿＿

4. Correct either the reading or writing mistakes in the following words.

大工	だいこう	作家	さくか	羽	はん
目曜日	もくようび	朝市	ちょうし	昼食	ちゃしょく
楽園	がくえん	星空	ほしそら	正牛	しょうご

Answers to exercises　練習解答

1. (Check them in the corresponding kanji tables #141, #142, #144, and #148.)
2. a) 原作: 2 | 深夜: 2 // b) 音楽: 3 | 天才: 1 | 新作: 3 // c) 工事: 3 | 日曜日: 4
3. つくりばなし: 作り話, made-up story | かようび: 火曜日, Tuesday
   あさひ: 朝日, Asahi | かせい: 火星, Mars
   ぎゅうにく: 牛肉, beef or veal | やがく: 夜学, night school
4. 大工 だいく | 作家 さっか | 羽 はね | 木曜日 もくようび
   朝市 あさいち | 昼食 ちゅうしょく | 楽園 らくえん | 星空 ほしぞら | 正午 しょうご

Manga translation　マンガ翻訳

Presenter: ...And so, this Sunday at noon, the spaceship built in a Japanese factory is scheduled to spread its wings and depart, bound for Mars.

Scientist: Colonel Yamada, all preparations are ready, but...

Scientist: It has not been decided yet who will be the pilot.

Scientist: Those are the main candidates.

Scientist (offscreen): They are both geniuses, and they are as healthy as oxen. They spend the whole day training, from morning to night.

Colonel: I see. It's not an easy choice. There's no alternative: they must pass the final test!

Scientist: The... the final test? Are you sure?

Astronauts (both at once): Rock, paper scissors! Rock, paper scissors!!

Workmates: Wow! Wow! Come on!

Scientist (thinking): There might be no alternative, but I still believe this is shameful...

New elements　新しい部首

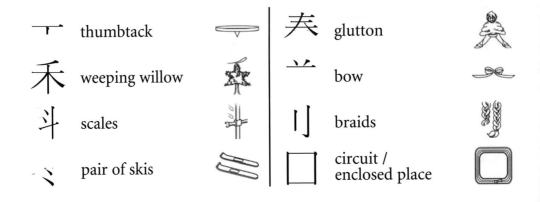

丁 thumbtack

禾 weeping willow

斗 scales

⺀ pair of skis

夫 glutton

丷 bow

刂 braids

囗 circuit / enclosed place

Lesson 14
第十四課

149 (3級)

SUMMER

カ

夏季 (か き) summer, summertime
初夏 (しょ か) early summer

なつ

夏 (なつ) summer
真夏 (ま なつ) midsummer
夏雲 (なつ ぐも) summer clouds
夏休み (なつ やす) summer holidays

(10 strokes)

注 息 (3rd)

学 What happens in *summer*? All eyes are fixed, like this a thumbtack, on the swimmer of the moment.

特 夒 (alt)

150 (2級)

WHEAT, BARLEY, OATS

バク

麦価 (ばく か) wheat price
麦秋 (ばく しゅう) barley harvest time
麦芽 (ばく が) malt

むぎ

小麦 (こ むぎ) wheat
麦茶 (むぎ ちゃ) barley tea
大麦 (おお むぎ) barley
ライ麦 (むぎ) rye

(7 strokes)

注 青 (36)

学 *Wheat* is the plant with which bread is made of. It is also the basis of a top-class swimmer's diet, rich in carbohydrates.

特 麥 (old)

151

FRIEND （4級）

(4 strokes)

ユウ
友人 friend(s)
親友 close friend
友情 friendship
僚友 colleague

とも
友 friend
友達 friend(s)
住友 Sumitomo (surname)

特

学 A good *friend* will use chopsticks if necessary to take his friend, the swimmer, out of the water. **Be careful** with the swimmer: his arms are against his body.

注 左 (75)
反 (3rd)

151

152

AUTUMN （3級）

(9 strokes)

シュウ
秋色 autumn colors
秋分 autumnal equinox
春夏秋冬 the four seasons

あき
秋 autumn
秋田 Akita (surname / place name)
秋晴れ(の日) beautiful autumn (day)
秋葉原 Akihabara (place)

特 烑 (alt)
穐 (alt)
龝 (alt)

学 The weeping willow cries in the *autumn* because it knows that all plan life around will soon dry up, and become easily susceptible to fire.

注 私 (6th)
秩 (Jōyō)

153 (2級)

DEPARTMENT, SUBJECT

カ

科目 subject
百科事典 encyclopedia
外科 surgery
内科 internal medicine
理科 (dept. of) science
分科 (dept. of) liberal arts
金科玉条 golden rule

科

(9 strokes)

注 秒 (3rd)
利 (4th)

学 The weeping willow cries when it weighs itself at the *department*'s scales, and realizes it hasn't lost one gram.

特

154 (2級)

NUMBER, ORDER

バン

番号 number, figure
一番 first, number 1, the most, the best
番組 (TV or radio) program
出番 one's turn
交番 police box
番犬 watchdog

番

(12 strokes)

注 雷 (Jōyō)

学 Planting grains of rice in the field, one by one, in *order*, takes sweat and tears.

特

155

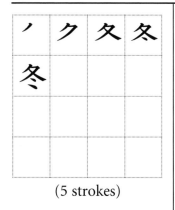

(5 strokes)

WINTER

(3級)

トウ
冬期 wintertime
冬季 winter season
冬眠 hibernation

ふゆ
冬 winter
真冬 midwinter
冬休み winter vacation
冬日 winter day(s)

 鼕 (old)

学 The swimmer adapts himself to everything: in *winter* he puts on skis, and he's ready to go!

注 寒 (3rd)
尽 (Jōyō)

156

(9 strokes)

SPRING

(3級)

シュン
春色 spring colors
春分 vernal equinox
青春 adolescence
売春 prostitution

はる
春 spring
春巻 spring roll
春風 spring breeze

学 As soon as *spring* arrives, the glutton Kim goes out to tan his rolls of fat in the sun.

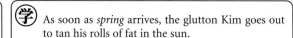

 奏 (6th)
香 (Jōyō)

157 (4級) — BEHIND, AFTER

ゴ
- 午後 (ご・ご) afternoon
- 前後 (ぜん・ご) before and after

コウ
- 後半 (こう・はん) second part / half

うし(ろ)
- 後ろ (うし・ろ) behind

あと
- 後で (あと) after, later on
- 後回し (あと・まわ) to postpone

(9 strokes)

注 徒 (4th)
　　従 (6th)

学 This picture shows what's *behind* the car in the highway: it's the swimmer, towed by thread. (Be careful with the "thread," it uses only the balls of yarn.)

特 后 (alt)

158 (4級) — BEFORE, FRONT

ゼン
- 午前 (ご・ぜん) morning
- 前日 (ぜん・じつ) the other day
- 前半 (ぜん・はん) first part / half

まえ
- 前に (まえ) before / in front of
- 五年前 (ご・ねん・まえ) five years ago
- 前戻し (まえ・もど) to go back
- 名前 (な・まえ) name

(9 strokes)

注 型 (4th)

学 Notice how the moon does herself up, with a magnificent bow and a pair of long braids, *before* her big night.

特 前 (alt)
　　拜 (alt)

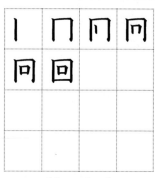

(6 strokes)

TO TURN, TIMES

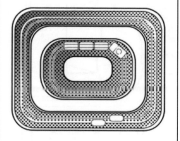

カイ
前回 last time (ぜんかい)
今回 this time (こんかい)
回転寿司 (かいてんずし)
sushi rotatory bar

まわ(る/す)
回る to turn around (まわ)
歩き回る to walk about (ある まわ)
回す to send around (まわ)

特 廻 (alt) 周 (hom) 囲 (alt)

学 How many times does your car *turn* in the circuit Grand Prix?

注 図 (183) 固 (4th)

155

(8 strokes)

ROCK

ガン
火山岩 volcanic rock (かざんがん)
岩塩 rock salt (がんえん)
溶岩 lava (ようがん)

いわ
岩 rock (いわ)
岩屋 cavern, cave (いわや)
岩手 Iwate (prefecture) (いわて)
岩井 Iwai (surname) (いわい)

特 嵒 (alt) 巌 (hom)

学 *Rock:* said of the gigantic rock supporting the mountain.

注 岸 (3rd) 炭 (3rd)

昔々、あるところに…

ほらほら！キツネじゃないの、それ!?あっ！岩に足が挟まれたのね…か？

あっ、そうだ！きっと、この娘はあの日に会った化けたキツネだ！へへ…ちょっとからかってやろうか？

ありがとう、友達！あんたはとても優しい人間だ！一番だ！二回目に会ったら、恩返しをしてあげよう！キツネにとっての金科玉条なんだ！

ああっ！しゃべった！

それから、春夏秋冬を繰り返した。ある日…

コンコン

はい、はい。

失礼いたします。わたくしは迷子になった旅人でございます。お水を飲ませてくださいませんか？

ま、水より麦茶はどうだ？でも、その前、キスしてもらおうね。

ナ・ナ…何言ってるの？

やれやれ…完ぺきに化けたな！後ろにしっぽもない？

こんにちは、友達！はい、恩返しだ、このおにぎり！うれしいだろう!?

Exercises 練習

1. Develop the stroke order of the following kanji.

夏									
番									
春									
後									

2. Choose the correct reading for each kanji or kanji combination.

a) あなた、<u>冬眠</u>する気？<u>一緒</u>に<u>街</u>を<u>歩き回る</u>って<u>約束</u>じゃなかったの！？

Are you planning to hibernate? Didn't you promise we would go for a walk in the city together?!

冬眠：　　1．とみん　　　　2．とうみん　　　　3．ふゆみん　　　4．ゆふみん

歩き回る：1．あきまわる　　2．あるきかいる　3．あるきまわる　4．あるきまわする

b) <u>秋色</u>ってきれいですね！ここまで<u>火山岩</u>を<u>登り</u>きるのは<u>大変</u>だったけどね。

Autumn colors are beautiful, aren't they?! But climbing this volcanic rock this far was hard.

秋色：　　1．あきしょく　2．あきいろ　　　3．しゅうしょ　　4．しゅうしょく

火山岩：　1．かざんがん　2．かさんがん　　3．かざんいわ　　4．かさんいわ

c) <u>前日</u>に、<u>番組</u>を見ていた<u>時</u>に、<u>青春</u><u>時代</u>の<u>友達</u>がテレビに出ていた。

The other day, when I was watching a program, a friend from my adolescence was on TV.

前日：　1．まえにち　　　2．まえび　　　　3．ぜんにち　　　4．ぜんじつ

番組：　1．ばくみ　　　　2．ばんくみ　　　3．ばんぐみ　　　4．ばぐみ

青春：　1．せいしゅん　　2．あおはる　　　3．せいしゅ　　　4．あおばる

友達：　1．ゆうだち　　　2．ゆうたち　　　3．ともだち　　　4．ともたち

3. Write the kanji (one or more) and the meaning of the following words.

なつやすみ　_____ _____　　　かもく　　　　_____ _____

でばん　　　_____ _____　　　ばいしゅん　_____ _____

ぜんご　　　_____ _____　　　なまえ　　　_____ _____

4. Correct either the reading or writing mistakes in the following words.

後回し	あともどし	前戻し	まえまわし	後	うしろ
真冬	まぶゆ	文番	こうばん	石手	いわて
春秋	ばくしゅう	少麦	こむぎ	初夏	しょなつ

Answers to exercises 練習解答

1. (Check them in the corresponding kanji tables #149, #154, #156, and #157.)

2. a) 冬眠: 2 | 歩き回る: 3 // b) 秋色: 4 | 火山岩: 1 // c) 前日: 4 | 番組: 3 | 青春: 1 | 友達: 3

3. なつやすみ: 夏休み, summer holidays | かもく: 科目, subject | でばん: 出番, one's turn
　　ばいしゅん: 売春, prostitution | ぜんご: 前後 before and after | なまえ: 名前, name

4. 後回し あとまわし | 前戻し まえもどし | 後ろ うしろ
　　真冬 まふゆ | 交番 こうばん | 岩手 いわて
　　麦秋 ばくしゅう or 春秋 しゅんじゅう | 小麦 こむぎ | 初夏 しょか

Manga translation マンガ翻訳

Text panel: Once upon a time, a very long time ago...
Youth: Fancy that! It's a fox! Oh... it looks like its leg is trapped by the rocks.
Fox: Thank you so much, my friend! You are a very kind human! The best! Next time we meet, I'll reward you! This is a golden rule for us, foxes!
Youth: It can talk! / **Text panel:** Then, one season followed another, until one day...
Sound of the door: Knock, knock / **Youth:** Yes, coming.
Princess: Excuse me, I'm a traveler and I got lost. Could you give me some water?
Youth: Of course! I'm sure this girl is the fox I met the other day, now transformed. Hee, hee, I'm going to pull her leg a little. / **Youth:** OK... Rather than water, would you prefer barley tea? But, before that, give me a kiss, come on.
Princess: B-b-but... what are you saying?! / **Youth:** Well I must say, you sure have transformed yourself well... You don't even have a tail behind?
Princess: Waaaah!! Don't be rude! / **Fox:** Hello, my friend! Here's your promised reward, a rice ball! Are you pleased? / **Sound behind the princess:** Grrrrr

New elements 新しい部首

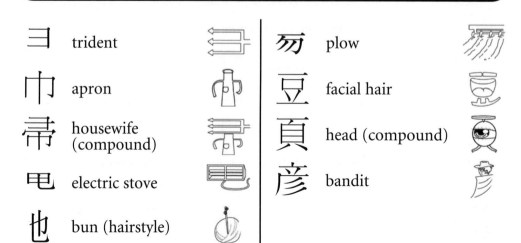

彐	trident		刕	plow	
巾	apron		豆	facial hair	
帚	housewife (compound)		頁	head (compound)	
电	electric stove		彦	bandit	
也	bun (hairstyle)				

Lesson 15
第十五課

161 (2級)

TO HIT THE MARK

トウ

とうぜん
当然 natural, obvious
べんとう
弁当 lunch box
ほんとう
本当 truth
てきとう
適当 suitable, adequate

あ(たる)

あ
当たる to hit the mark
あ　　まえ
当たり前 logical, obvious
こころあ
心当たり to have an idea
about, to have a clue

(6 strokes)

注 雪 (162)
　 争 (4th)

学 The dwarf alone has the skill to always *hit the mark* with the trident, his favorite weapon.

特 當 (alt)

160

162 (2級)

SNOW

セツ

しんせつ
新雪 fresh snow
こうせつ
降雪 snowfall
ごうせつ
豪雪 heavy snowfall

ゆき

ゆき
雪 snow
ゆき　　ふ
雪が降る to snow
ゆき おとこ
雪男 the Yeti
ゆきがっせん
雪合戦 snowball fight
ゆき
雪だるま snowman

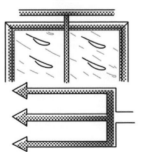

(11 strokes)

注 電 (165)
　 雲 (164)
　 雷 (Jōyō)

学 *Snow* is the only kind of "rain" in which the trident can stick itself into.

特 雪 (alt)

163 (3級) TO RETURN

	リ	ﾘ	ﾘｰ
ﾘｰ	ﾘ゠	ﾘ゠	帰
帰	帰		

(10 strokes)

| 帰 | 帰 | **帰** | 帰 |
| 帰 | 帰 | 帰 | **帰** |

キ
帰国 (きこく) to return
　　to one's country
社会復帰 (しゃかいふっき) reintegrated
　　into society

かえ（る）
帰る (かえる) to return
　　to go back home
お帰りなさい (かえ)
　　"Welcome back!"
帰り道 (かえ みち) the way back (home)
日帰り (ひがえ) a one-day (trip)

学 Braids are the *return* to childhood for the housewife (on the right): she was a ballerina, but has traded her tutu in for an apron, and now rules her house, trident in hand.

注 帚 (Jōyō)
　　婦 (5th)
　　帯 (4th)

164 (2級) CLOUD

一	一	一	二
一	一	一	二
雨	雨	雲	雲

(12 strokes)

| 雲 | 雲 | **雲** | 雲 |
| 雲 | 雲 | 雲 | **雲** |

ウン
暗雲 (あんうん) dark clouds
星雲 (せいうん) nebula

くも
雲 (くも) cloud
雲行き (くも ゆ) weather, the look
　　of the sky; the situation
雲隠れ (くも がく) to disappear
　　(into thin air)
雨雲 (あまぐも) rain clouds

学 What is a *cloud*? A feast of rain (and when it can't bear it any longer, it lets it go).

注 電 (165)
　　雪 (162)
　　零 (Jōyō)

165 (4級) ELECTRICITY

デン

でんき
電気 electricity
でんち
電池 battery
かいちゅうでんとう
懐中電灯 flashlight
でんしゃ
電車 train
でんわ
電話 telephone
でんきゅう
電球 light bulb
でんこう
電光 electric light
でんし
電子 electron

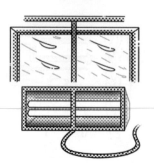

(13 strokes)

注 雪 (162)
　　雲 (164)
　　雷 (Jōyō)

学 Here you have an electric stove. In the rain, *electricity* can cause serious trouble.

特

166 (2級) LIFE, ACTIVITY

カツ

せいかつ
生活 life
せいかつようしき
生活様式 lifestyle
し　せいかつ
私生活 private life
かつりょく
活力 energy, vitality
かつどう
活動 activity
かつどうか
活動家 activist

い(きる)

い
活きる to live, to exist
い　ばな
生け花 flower arrangement

(9 strokes)

注 舌 (5th)
　　治 (4th)
　　乱 (6th)

学 Imagine the frenzied *activity* of one thousand mouths splashing the water about.

特

167

STEAM

(1級)

(7 strokes)

汽

キ
汽車 (きしゃ) train run by steam
汽船 (きせん) steamship
汽圧 (きあつ) steam pressure
汽笛 (きてき) steam whistle
汽艇 (きてい) steam launch

特

学 Condensed water, turned into *steam*, causes fog.

注 気 (52)
池 (168)

168

POND

(3級)

(6 strokes)

池

チ
乾電池 (かんでんち) battery, dry cell
太陽電池 (たいようでんち) solar battery
光電池 (こうでんち) photoelectric cell
貯水池 (ちょすいち) reservoir

いけ
池 (いけ) pond
人工池 (じんこういけ) artificial pond
古池 (ふるいけ) old pond

特

学 If your hair bun were water, it would be a swirling *pond*.

注 地 (169)
他 (3rd)
也 (Jōyō)

169 (3級)

EARTH, LAND

チ
地球 (ちきゅう) the Earth
土地 (とち) land
地下鉄 (ちかてつ) subway
地理 (ちり) geography

ジ
地色 (じいろ) ground-color
地獄 (じごく) hell
地震 (じしん) earthquake

一	十	土	地
地	地		

(6 strokes)

地	也	**地**	地
地	地	地	**地**

(注) 池 (168)
他 (3rd)
也 (Jōyō)

(学) If your hair bun were fertile *land*, it would be the *earth* of a small raked japanese garden.

(特)

---

170 (3級)

PLACE

ジョウ
会場 (かいじょう) grounds, site
工場 (こうじょう) factory
欠場 (けつじょう) to fail to show up

ば
場所 (ばしょ) place
現場 (げんば) on the scene
場合 (ばあい) case, situation
広場 (ひろば) public square
乗り場 (のりば) (taxi) stand, (bus) stop

一	十	土	圹
圹	圹	圹	坦
圹	堨	場	場

(12 strokes)

場	場	**場**	場
場	場	場	**場**

(注) 易 (5th), 湯 (3rd), 揚 (Jōyō), 陽 (3rd), 傷 (6th)

(学) The ideal *place* for cultivation is a patch of fertile land in the sun, with a rake to work it.

(特) 場 (alt)

171

HEAD (3級)

(16 strokes)

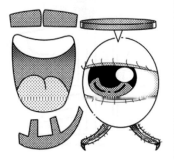

トウ

先頭 (in the) lead, at the head
せんとう

出頭 attendance
しゅっとう

初頭 beginning
しょとう

巨頭 leader, magnate
きょとう

頭骨 skull
とうこつ

あたま

頭 head
あたま

石頭 stubborn, hard head
いし あたま

特

学 To the right, the picture of the component *head*: a shell stuck with a thumbtack. To the left, the facial hair characteristics of the head of the family.

注 題 (3rd)
顔 (172)
頂 (6th)

172

FACE (3級)

顔

(18 strokes)

ガン

童顔 childish face
どうがん

かお

顔 face
かお

笑顔 smiling face
え がお

泣き顔 tearful face
な がお

顔を売れる to be well known
かお う

新顔 new face, newcomer
しんがお

横顔 profile
よこがお

特 顔 (old)

学 The WANTED posters are all over the city. In them is the bandit's *face*, for whose head a substantial reward is offered.

注 題 (3rd)
親 (180)
頭 (171)

Exercises 練習

1. Develop the stroke order of the following kanji.

池						
場						
頭						
顔						

2. Choose the correct reading for each kanji or kanji combination.

a) 何、その泣き顔！？雪合戦していたら、頭に投げられるのは当然でしょう？

What's that tearful face?! In a snowball fight, getting hit on the head is normal, isn't it?

泣き顔: 1．なきかお 2．なきがお 3．なきがん 4．なきかん

雪合戦: 1．せつがっせん 2．せっがっせん 3．ゆきがせん 4．ゆきがっせん

頭: 1．かお 2．がお 3．たあま 4．あたま

当然: 1．あたぜん 2．あたりぜん 3．とうぜん 4．とぜん

b) 地震の場合、電気を消し、テーブルの下に隠れてください。

In case of an earthquake, switch off the electricity and hide under a table.

地震: 1．ちしん 2．ちじん 3．じじん 4．じしん

場合: 1．ばあい 2．ばごう 3．じょうごう 4．じょうあい

電気: 1．でんけ 2．でんき 3．てんけ 4．てんき

c) 雨雲が見えてきたから、今日は歩かない。地下鉄で帰りましょう。

Since I see rain clouds, today I won't walk. I'll take the subway home.

雨雲: 1．あめぐも 2．あめくも 3．あまぐも 4．ううん

地下鉄: 1．じかてつ 2．しかてつ 3．づかてつ 4．ちかてつ

3. Write the kanji (one or more) and the meaning of the following words.

ほんとう	_____ _____	ゆきおとこ	_____ _____
ひがえり	_____ _____	いけばな	_____ _____
きしゃ	_____ _____	ひろば	_____ _____

4. Correct either the reading or writing mistakes in the following words.

工場	こうば	地獄	ちこく	当たり後	あたりまえ
出頭	しゅっと	弛	いけ	お帰なさい	おかえりなさい

Answers to exercises 練習解答

1. (Check them in the corresponding kanji tables #168, #170, #171, and #172.)

2. a) 泣き顔: 2｜雪合戦: 4｜頭: 4｜当然: 3

   b) 地震: 4｜場合: 1｜電気: 2 // c) 雨雲: 3｜地下鉄: 4

3. ほんとう: 本当, truth｜ゆきおとこ: 雪男, the Yeti｜ひがえり: 日帰り, one-day trip｜いけばな: 生け花, flower arrangement｜きしゃ: 汽車, train run by steam｜ひろば: 広場, public square

4. 工場 こうじょう｜地獄 じごく｜当たり前 あたりまえ

   出頭 しゅっとう｜池 いけ｜お帰りなさい おかえりなさい

Manga translation マンガ翻訳

Policeman: Oh, it has been an unfortunate accident.

Voice: I'm sorry, but I disagree. We are before an obvious case of murder.

Policeman (offscreen): The famous detective Sherlock Holmes!!

Holmes: That's right. / Let's investigate the scene of the crime. Hmm... Water, and this reddish earth... I see. / According to the deceased's habits, it seems he went out every morning for a walk. However, since it was snowing today, he came home straight away. / (offscreen) Due to the clouds, it was very dark, and the criminal had also switched off the electricity. He had even hidden the batteries for the flashlight. Therefore, the victim stumbled and hit himself on the head. Consequently... / (onscreen) The murderer... is the butler!!

Policeman: Fantastic, Holmes! Your deductive method is impressive. But...

Policeman: ...In this day and age, neither batteries nor electric light nor anything of the kind has been invented yet! We are still in the age of steam locomotives, you fool!!

Holmes: Hmm... Elementary.

New elements 新しい部首

自	I		𣎳	cowboy handkerchief	
首	neck		羊	guard	
辶	road		由	bucket	
吉	masked man (compound)		凵	frame	
斤	steam iron				

Lesson　16
第十六課

173 (3級)

I, SELF-, ONESELF

ジ

自分 (じぶん) oneself
自慢 (じまん) pride
自由 (じゆう) freedom
自殺 (じさつ) suicide
自動車 (じどうしゃ) motor vehicle
自転車 (じてんしゃ) bicycle
自信 (じしん) self-confidence
自動販売機 (じどうはんばいき)
vending machine

(6 strokes)

注 目 (22)
　 白 (37)

学 Because *I*'m worth it.

特

---

174 (3級)

NECK

シュ

自首 (じしゅ) surrender
絞首刑 (こうしゅけい) execution
　　　　by hanging
首都 (しゅと) capital city
首相 (しゅしょう) prime minister

くび

首 (くび) neck
手首 (てくび) wrist
足首 (あしくび) ankle
乳首 (ちくび) nipple

(9 strokes)

注 道 (175)
　 百 (38)
　 音 (43)

学 The giraffe with the long *neck* has a magnificent bow decorating its eye.

特

(12 strokes)

WAY, ROAD

(4級) **175**

ドウ
歩道 footpath
水道 waterworks
武道 martial arts
海道 coastal route
茶道 tea ceremony
武士道 *bushidō*
(the way of the samurai)

みち
道 road
近道 shortcut

特 道 (alt)
衜 (alt)

学 The long-necked giraffe goes down the *road* on its *way*. Radical: 辶.

注 首 (174)
週 (175)

(11 strokes)

WEEK

(4級) **176**

シュウ
今週 this week
先週 last week
来週 next week
一週間 one week's time
何週間 several weeks
週末 weekend
週刊 weekly publication

特

学 The masked man's road: the entire *week* disguised in his fertile land mask and his wig, hoping not to be discovered...

注 周 (4th)
道 (175)

177 (3級)

FAR

エン
- 永遠 (えいえん) eternity
- 遠心力 (えんしんりょく) centrifugal force
- 遠足 (えんそく) excursion
- 望遠鏡 (ぼうえんきょう) telescope
- 遠慮 (えんりょ) reserve, modesty

とお(い)
- 遠い (とお) distant, far
- 遠回し (とおまわ) roundabout way

一	十	土	𠮷
吉	吉	袁	袁
袁	袁	袁	遠
遠			

(13 strokes)

(注) 園 (181)
違 (Jōyō)
猿 (Jōyō)

(学) When his disguise fails, the masked man changes his wig for a cowboy handkerchief, and escapes: he goes *far* along the road.

(特) 逺 (alt)

178 (3級)

NEAR, CLOSE

キン
- 近所 (きんじょ) neighborhood
- 近辺 (きんぺん) vicinity
- 近親 (きんしん) close relative
- 近眼 (きんがん) nearsightedness
- 近代 (きんだい) nowadays
- 最近 (さいきん) lately
- 近作 (きんさく) recent work

ちか(い)
- 近い (ちか) near, close

| 一 | 厂 | 斤 | 斤 |
| 斤 | 近 | 近 | |

(7 strokes)

(注) 斤 (Jōyō)
返 (3rd)

(学) *Close* up, the wrinkles on the road are obvious: we must iron them out.

(特)

179

NEW

、	亠	产	立
立	立	辛	辛
辛	辛	新	新
新			

(13 strokes)

シン
新聞 (しんぶん) newspaper
更新 (こうしん) to renew, to renovate
最新 (さいしん) the latest
新婚 (しんこん) just married
新車 (しんしゃ) new car
新緑 (しんりょく) fresh vegetables
新幹線 (しんかんせん) bullet-train

あたら(しい)
新しい (あたら) new

特

学 Look at the vulture on the tree: from now on, it will personify a guard. In this case, he is a modern one, who, instead of a gun, has a *new* weapon: the iron.

注 親 (180)

180

PARENTS, RELATIVES

、	亠	产	立
立	立	辛	辛
亲	亲	新	親
親	親	親	親

(16 strokes)

シン
親族 (しんぞく) relatives
親切 (しんせつ) kindness

おや
親 (おや) father / mother
父親 (ちちおや) father
親子 (おやこ) parents and children
親指 (おやゆび) thumb

した(しい)
親しい (した) close, friendly

特

学 Sometimes, our *parents* seem like guards who constantly watch us.

注 新 (179)
顔 (172)

181 (2級)

PARK, GARDEN

エン

公園 public park
学園 campus
幼稚園 kindergarten
動物園 zoo
植物園 botanical garden
国立公園 national park
楽園 paradise

その

園 garden, park

(13 strokes)

 遠 (177)
固 (4th)
国 (182)

 A *park* is the enclosed place where the fleeing masked man rests, with his cowboy scarf.

 薗 (alt)

182 (4級)

COUNTRY

コク

王国 monarchy
民主国 democratic country
国民 a nation, a people
母国語 mother tongue
外国 foreign country
売国 betrayal of one's country
中国 China

くに

国 country

(8 strokes)

 玉 (16)
図 (183)

 Which is the enclosed place where the king can play ball as much as he wants? His *country*, of course.

國 (old)
囯 (alt)

183

PLAN, DIAGRAM (3級)

(7 strokes)

ズ
地図 plan, map
合図 symbol, sign
図表 diagram, graphic

ト
図書館 library
意図 intention, purpose
企図 plan, project

はか（る）
図る to plan, to design

 特　圖 (old)

学　*Plan*: diagram of an enclosed place where you can measure every inch of terrain with scales.

注　囲 (4th)
団 (5th)
困 (6th)

184

DRAWING, STROKE (3級)

(8 strokes)

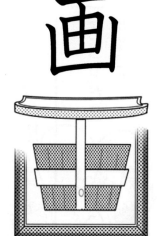

ガ
映画 movie
映画館 cinema (building)
漫画 comic-book, manga
漫画家 manga author
画家 painter, artist
絵画 painting

カク
計画 plan, project, program

 特　畫 (alt)
畵 (alt)

学　My first *drawing* was basic: a slice of bread and the bucket we use to draw water from the well. My mom was so happy that she framed it on the wall.

注　面 (3rd)
再 (5th)

Exercises　練習

1. Develop the stroke order of the following kanji.

道						
遠						
近						
画						

2. Choose the correct reading for each kanji or kanji combination.

a) 一週間ずっと勉強してきたのに、合格する自信はゼロだ。

Even though I've been studying non-stop for one week, my self-confidence for passing is still zero.

一週間：　1．いしゅうかん　2．いしゅかん　　3．いっしゅかん　4．いっしゅうかん

自信：　1．ちじん　　　2．しじん　　　3．じしん　　　4．じじん

b) 親子関係を大切にしている人は、子供を連れて動物園や映画館や公園などへ行く。

Those who value parent-child relationships take their children to the zoo, the movies, or the park.

親子：　　1．しんこ　　　2．しんし　　　3．おやこ　　　4．おやし

動物園：　1．どうぶつぜん　2．どうぶつえん　3．どうぶつその　4．どうぶつぞの

映画館：　1．えいかかん　　2．えいかくかん　3．えいかっかん　4．えいがかん

公園：　　1．こうえん　　　2．おおやぞの　　3．こうぞの　　　4．ひろぞの

c) 地図を忘れたぁ！？道迷っちゃうよ！首都ははじめてだもん！

You have forgotten the map?! We'll get lost! This is my first time in the capital!

地図：　1．じと　　　2．ちと　　　3．じず　　　4．ちず

首都：　1．しゅと　　2．しゅうと　　3．しゅっと　　4．しっと

3. Write the kanji (one or more) and the meaning of the following words.

じぶん　　　_____ _____　　あしくび　　_____ _____

ちかみち　　_____ _____　　せんしゅう　_____ _____

しんしゃ　　_____ _____　　がいこく　　_____ _____

4. Correct either the reading or writing mistakes in the following words.

首自	じしゅ	武首	ぶどう	園足	えんそく
金所	きんじょ	新い	あたらしい	親切	しせつ
楽園	らくぞの	図かる	はかる	計画	けいが

Answers to exercises 練習解答

1. (Check them in the corresponding kanji tables #175, #177, #178, and #184)

2. a) 一週間: 4 | 自信: 3 // b) 親子: 3 | 動物園: 2 | 映画館: 4 | 公園: 1 // c) 地図: 4 | 首都: 1

3. じぶん: 自分, oneself | あしくび: 足首, ankle

ちかみち: 近道, shortcut | せんしゅう: 先週, last week

しんしゃ: 新車, new car | がいこく: 外国, foreign country

4. 自首 じしゅ | 武道 ぶどう | 遠足 えんそく | 近所 きんじょ | 新しい あたらしい

親切 しんせつ | 楽園 らくえん | 図る はかる | 計画 けいかく

Manga translation マンガ翻訳

Bounty hunter: I'm getting closer! According to this map, the treasure is somewhere around here!

Bounty hunter: Ha, ha, ha, ha! With this, I'll be able to buy a new house..., no! My own castle even!

Imp: Hang on! This treasure is mine!

Bounty hunter: What?! Is this a kindergarten or what? Listen carefully, you shrimp. I come from a distant country and I've been on the road for weeks...

Imp: Let me go!

Bounty hunter: ...To get this treasure. If you don't want me to cut your head off, be good and get lost, OK?

Imp: Daaaad!

Father devil: What's going on here? Is there a problem?

Bounty hunter: No, no, none. In fact, I was just leaving...

Bounty hunter (thinking): W-what the hell is this!? This is just like a manga!

New elements 新しい部首

用	moon with rope to go down	开	torii (shrine gate)
マ	magician's hat	彡	folds, wrinkles
ク	camera flash	可	lottery stand window
巴	scuba goggles	欠	drunk Kim

Lesson　17
第十七課

185 (3級)

TO USE

ヨウ

用 business
<ruby>用<rt>よう</rt></ruby>

使用 use, application
<ruby>使用<rt>しよう</rt></ruby>

利用者 user
<ruby>利用者<rt>りようしゃ</rt></ruby>

常用 everyday use
<ruby>常用<rt>じょうよう</rt></ruby>

日用品 daily necessities
<ruby>日用品<rt>にちようひん</rt></ruby>

用心 care, caution
<ruby>用心<rt>ようじん</rt></ruby>

もち(いる)

用いる to use
<ruby>用<rt>もち</rt></ruby>いる

(5 strokes)

注 冊 (6th)
角 (187)

学 The moon *uses* a rope to come down from the sky to visit us.

特

186 (3級)

TO GO THROUGH, TO PASS

ツウ

交通 traffic
<ruby>交通<rt>こうつう</rt></ruby>

普通 normal, common
<ruby>普通<rt>ふつう</rt></ruby>

通信 communication
<ruby>通信<rt>つうしん</rt></ruby>

通信社 news agency
<ruby>通信社<rt>つうしんしゃ</rt></ruby>

通学 to attend school
<ruby>通学<rt>つうがく</rt></ruby>

とお(る)

通る to go through, to pass
<ruby>通<rt>とお</rt></ruby>る

大通り avenue
<ruby>大通<rt>おおどお</rt></ruby>り

かよ(う)

通う to commute
<ruby>通<rt>かよ</rt></ruby>う

(10 strokes)

注 連 (4th)
角 (187)
進 (3rd)

学 The moon disguises itself with a magician's hat to *pass* through the crowd and go on its way.

特 通 (alt)

(7 strokes)

CORNER, ANGLE, HORN

(2級)

187

カク
角度 angle
三角形 triangle
四角 square
直角 right angle

かど
角 corner
街角 street corner

つの
角 horn

(特) 角 (alt)
角 (alt)

(学) The moon, with a camera flash strapped to her head like a *horn*, has come down to take photos from every angle, and hides around *corners* so as not to be seen.

(注) 用 (185)
通 (186)

(6 strokes)

COLOR

(2級)

188

ショク
原色 primary color
好色 sensuality

いろ
色 color
金色 golden color
茶色 light brown
肌色 flesh-colored
色々 various
顔色 complexion,
     expression

(特)

(学) To appreciate the *colors* at the bottom of the sea you need a camera with a flash, and diving goggles.

(注) 免 (not Jōyō)
声 (112)
巴 (not Jōyō)

189 (2級)

SHAPE, FORM

ケイ
えんけい
円形 round
げんけい
原形 original form
ずけい
図形 figure
じけい
字形 font, typography
けいしき
形式 formula, formality
むけい
無形 abstract, intangible

かたち
かたち
形 form

| 一 | 二 | 干 | 开 |
| 开 | 形 | 形 | |

(7 strokes)

形 形 **形** 形
形 形 形 **形**

(注) 刑 (Jōyō)
型 (4th)
杉 (Jōyō)

(学) Have you ever seen a torii, the entrance to a Shinto shrine? It has a sacred *form*, immune to the folds and wrinkles that betray the passing of time.

(特) 形 (alt)

190 (3級)

BODY

タイ
ぐたいてき
具体的 concretely
はんどうたい
半導体 semiconductor
こたい
固体 a solid
きたい
気体 a gas
したい
死体 corpse
せいたい
生体 living body, organism

からだ
からだ
体 body

| ノ | イ | 仁 | 什 |
| 什 | 休 | 体 | |

(7 strokes)

体 体 **体** 体
体 体 体 **体**

(注) 休 (61)

(学) The *body* is the basis of the person.

(特) 體 (old)
躰 (alt)
軆 (alt)

(7 strokes)

TO RUN

(3級) 191

ソウ
しゅっそう
出走 to participate in a race
きょうそう
競走 race
きょうそう ば
競走馬 racing horse
そうしゃ
走者 runner
だっそう
脱走 deserter, to flee

はし（る）
はし
走る to run
くちばし
口走る to blurt out, to let slip out

特 赱 (alt)

学 Athletes *run* on fertile land to get on the winner's tripod.

注 歩 (88)
足 (19)

THICK, FAT

(4 strokes)

(3級) 192

タイ
たいよう
太陽 the sun
たいへいよう
太平洋 Pacific ocean
たい こ
太鼓 drum

ふと（い/る）
ふと
太い thick, big
ふと
太る to put on weight
かたぶと
固太り person of solid build
ふと ま
太巻き a thick sushi roll

特

学 A *fat* and clumsy giant treads on the ball. He's different from the more skillful dog (48), who played with it.

注 大 (47)
犬 (48)

193 (4級)

HIGH, EXPENSIVE

コウ

最高 maximum, best
高価 high price
高温 high temperature
高校生 high school
　　　 student
高血圧 high blood
　　　 pressure

たか(い)

高い high, expensive
背が高い tall

、	亠	六	古
古	宁	高	高
高	高		

(10 strokes)

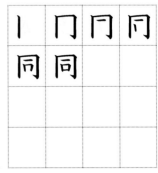

注 喜 (4th)

学 Look at the Mexican and his girlfriend at the opera: he is on a *higher* box, which was more *expensive*.

特

194 (3級)

SAME

同

ドウ

共同 cooperation, collective
同僚 colleague, associate
同士 companion
同性 homosexuality
同情 sympathy
同時 at the same time

おな(じ)

同じ same

丨	冂	冂	同
同	同		

(6 strokes)

注 向 (3rd)
　 何 (195)

学 In times of ration, we are all considered the *same*, and one slice of bread goes to each mouth.

特 仝 (alt)

195

(7 strokes)

WHAT?

(4級)

なに
何 what?
何か something
何も nothing

なん
何で why?
何となく somehow
何日 what day? how many days?
何千 several thousands

特

学 Our person Kim is waiting at the lottery stand window to see *what* he wins.

注 同 (194)
何 (Jōyō)

196

(14 strokes)

SONG, TO SING

(3級)

カ
国歌 national anthem
歌劇 opera
歌手 singer
歌詞 lyrics of a song
歌舞伎 *kabuki* theatre

うた/(う)
歌 song
歌う to sing

特 詞 (alt)

学 Having won the lottery not once but twice, Kim is drunk with glee; and, to celebrate, he *sings* to... a chair?!

注 飲 (3rd)

はい、
次の方
どうぞ。

ん？あの
角のかぶとを
かぶっている
デカ女を
見て！

背が
高いな〜！

何の用で来た
のかな、あの
太ったブス？

通路から
通られない
ぐらい
です！

そう、
そう！
体の形は
同じです
からね！

はっはっ
はっは

肌色が黒
なら、くじら
そっくり
だったな！

し…しかし、
歌が上手だし、
耳はするどいし…

そ…
そして
速く
走ります
ね…

とわわ〜っ！

186

Exercises 練習

1. Develop the stroke order of the following kanji.

用								
色								
走								
歌								

2. Choose the correct reading for each kanji or kanji combination.

a) 犯人は、固太りで、背が高い人に違いありません。

The murderer must be a tall man of solid build.

固太り： 1．かたふといり 2．かたふとり 3．かたぶといり 4．かたぶとり

背が高い：1．せがたかい 2．せがだかい 3．せがだい 4．せがこうい

b) 私は歌劇、旦那は競走馬: 高い趣味ばっかり！

Me, the opera; my husband, racing horses: we have expensive tastes!

歌劇： 1．かけき 2．かげき 3．うたけき 4．うたげき

競走馬： 1．きょうそば 2．きょうそうば 3．きょうはしば 4．きょうはしるば

c) 何で普通に話さないのか？おい、顔色が悪いぞ！

Why don't you talk normally? Hey, you look pale!

何で： 1．なにで 2．なにんで 3．なんで 4．なで

普通： 1．ふつ 2．ふうつ 3．ふつう 4．ふうつう

顔色： 1．がんしょく 2．かおしょく 3．かおいろ 4．がんいろ

3. Write the kanji (one or more) and the meaning of the following words.

とおる ＿＿＿＿ ＿＿＿＿ さんかくけい ＿＿＿＿ ＿＿＿＿

きんいろ ＿＿＿＿ ＿＿＿＿ からだ ＿＿＿＿ ＿＿＿＿

こうこうせい ＿＿＿＿ ＿＿＿＿ どうじ ＿＿＿＿ ＿＿＿＿

4. Correct either the reading or writing mistakes in the following words.

日曜品	にちようひん	交通	こうつ	原巴	げんしょく
街角	まちづの	刑	かたち	死休	したい
大い	ふとい	可	なに	歌たう	うたう

Answers to exercises 練習解答

1. (Check them in the corresponding kanji tables #185, #188, #191, and #196)

2. a) 固太り: 4 | 背が高い: 1 // b) 歌劇: 2 | 競走馬: 2 // c) 何で: 3 | 普通: 3 | 顔色: 3

3. とおる: 通る, to go through, to pass | さんかくけい: 三角形, triangle | きんいろ: 金色 golden color | からだ: 体, body | こうこうせい: 高校生, high school student | どうじ: 同時, at the same time, simultaneous

4. 日用品 にちようひん | 交通 こうつう | 原色 げんしょく | 街角 まちかど
形 かたち | 死体 したい | 太い ふとい | 何 なに | 歌を う うたう

Manga translation マンガ翻訳

Director: Very good... Next one.

Director: Hum? Look at the giant woman with the helmet with horns.

Assistant: She sure is tall..

Director: What has that fatso come here for?

Assistant: She probably can't even get through the aisles!

Director: If her skin were black, she would be a whale!

Director (out of the bubble): Ha, ha, ha, ha

Assistant: Yes, she would! Because her body shape is the same!

Assistant (out of the bubble): Ho, ho, ho, ho

Sound of swallowing hard: Gulp

Director: H-h-however, she sings really well... and she has very sharp hearing...

Assistant: And she sure can run...!

Onomatopoeia of scream, between both of them: Waaaah!

New elements 新しい部首

北 Northern Indians
南 Southern felines
西 Western swing doors
里 village

予 cowboy magician
市 market
ネ business woman
廾 fence

Lesson 18
第十八課

197 (4級) NORTH

ホク
ほっかい
北海 North Sea
ほっかいどう
北海道 Hokkaidō (island)
ほくせい
北西 northwest
ほくい
北緯 north latitude

きた
きた
北 north
きたぐち
北口 north exit
きたちょうせん
北朝鮮 North Korea

北

一	十	土	北
北			

(5 strokes)

北	北	**北**	北
北	北	北	**北**

 化 (3rd)
比 (5th)
此 (not Jōyō)

 These two Indians are from a tribe in the *north*.

特

---

198 (4級) SOUTH

ナン
なんべい
南米 South America
なんきょく
南極 South Pole,
the Antarctic
なんぴょうよう
南氷洋 Antarctic Ocean
なんぽう
南方 southward

みなみ
みなみ
南 south
みなみがわ
南側 south side

南

一	十	十	内
内	内	南	南
南			

(9 strokes)

南	南	**南**	南
南	南	南	**南**

 商 (3rd)

 And the devout felines are from the *south*.

特

199

EAST, ORIENT (4級)

(8 strokes)

トウ
とうよう
東洋 the Orient, the East
とうけい
東経 east longitude
とうざい
東西 east and west
とうざいなんぼく
東西南北 the four cardinal points
とうおう
東欧 Eastern Europe

ひがし
ひがし
東 east
ひがし がわ
東側 east side

 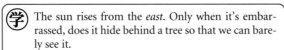

特 | 学 The sun rises from the *east*. Only when it's embarrassed, does it hide behind a tree so that we can barely see it. | 注 車 (32) / 東 (4th) / 末 (4th)

191

200

WEST, OCCIDENT (4級)

(6 strokes)

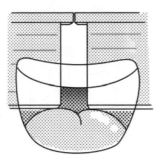

セイ
せいよう
西洋 the Occident
せいようじん
西洋人 a Westerner
たいせいよう
大西洋 Atlantic Ocean

サイ
かんさい
関西 Kansai (area)

にし
にし
西 west
にしぐち
西口 west exit

特 卤 (alt) | 学 The swing doors at the entrance of a saloon in the *West*. | 注 四 (11) / 酉 (not Jōyō) / 丙 (Jōyō)

201 (1級) VILLAGE, LEAGUE

リ

里 Japanese mile (about 2.44 miles)
海里 nautical mile

さと

里 village, hometown
村里 village
里心 homesickness
山里 mountain village
里人 villager

里

一 冂 冃 日
甲 甲 里

(7 strokes)

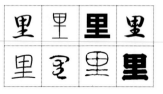

(注) 理 (224)
黒 (226)

(学) A *village* is strategically placed where there's fertile land to cultivate rice.

(特) 裡 (alt)

202 (3級) FIELD, CULTIVATION

ヤ

野生 wild
野菜 vegetable
野犬 stray dog
野球 baseball
視野 horizon

の

野原 field
野山 hills and fields
野放し as one pleases, leaving things to themselves

野

一 冂 冃 日
甲 甲 里 野
野 野 野

(11 strokes)

(注) 理 (224)

(学) Here is a cowboy magician who settles down in this village, and devotes the rest of his life to the *cultivation* of the fields.

(特) 埜 (alt)

203

MARKET, CITY　（3級）

| 、 | 一 | 亠 | 市 |
| 市 | | | |

(5 strokes)

シ
市 city
市長 mayor
市役所 city hall
市民 citizen/s

いち
市 market
市場 marketplace
見本市 trade fair

特

学 Who goes to the *market* early in the morning? The woman with her Mexican hat and her apron.

注 布 (5th)
巾 (not Jōyō)

204

CAPITAL, KYOTO　（3級）

| 、 | 一 | 亠 | 市 |
| 古 | 市 | 京 | 京 |

(8 strokes)

キョウ
東京 Tokyo
京都 Kyoto
京大 Kyoto University

Special
北京 Beijing
南京 Nanjing

特 京 (alt)

学 Rich kids in the *capital* are dwarves with big mouths and Mexican hats.

注 束 (4th)

205 (3級)

TEA

チャ

お茶 (green) tea
抹茶 (green) powdered tea
無茶苦茶 absurd, a mess, nonsensical
紅茶 black tea
茶の湯 tea ceremony
茶屋 teahouse
麦茶 barley tea

Special
喫茶店 tea room, coffee shop

(9 strokes)

 余 (5th)
英 (4th)

 A *tea* grower does the following: over the leaves, he places a cross so that God protects them, an umbrella in case it rains, and a crown of flowers to decorate them.

特

---

206 (4級)

COMPANY, SHINTO SHRINE

シャ

会社 company, corporation
株式会社 Inc.
社会 society
社長 company president
支社 branch office
社交 social life
神社 Shinto shrine

Special
社 Shinto shrine

(7 strokes)

注 社 (Jōyō)
祀 (not Jōyō)

学 This voluptuous business woman has found fertile land to create her *company* and make it thrive.

 社 (alt)

207

(14 strokes)

TO CALCULATE

サン

計算 calculation
加算 addition
引き算 subtraction
暗算 mental calculation
合算 total amount
予算 estimate
公算 probability
算数 arithmetic

 学 You need a sharp eye to *calculate* the number of bamboo canes there are in a fenced wood.

 注 鼻 (3rd)

195

208

(12 strokes)

TO ANSWER

(3級)

トウ

解答 solution
問答 questions and answers
回答 reply, response

こた(える)

答え answer
答える to answer
口答え retort, backtalk

 特   学 To the question, "What is bamboo?," the *answer* is: a group of canes!

 注 谷 (95)
合 (101)

我々の会社は世界中に知られている…

田舎の小さい村里から東京まで、どこの都市にも店を持っている…

全国の東西南北に支社がある…

それなのに、今年売られた自動車の合算は…ゼロだ!!どうして!?これを野放しにしてはいられない

お茶。我々が販売しているのはお茶です、社長。

そ・そうか…その答えがあった…

Exercises 練習

1. Develop the stroke order of the following kanji.

東								
野								
市								
社								

2. Choose the correct reading for each kanji or kanji combination.

a) 私の故 郷は日本の北西にある山里です。野菜がおいしいよ！

My hometown is a mountain village in the northwest of Japan. The vegetables there are delicious!

北西：1．ほくにち　　2．きたせい　　3．ほくせい　　4．きたにち

山里：1．さんり　　　2．やまり　　　3．やまさと　　4．やまざと

野菜：1．やざい　　　2．やせい　　　3．やさい　　　4．のざい

b) 市民の悩みに回答するのは僕の市長としての責任です。

Responding to the citizens' concerns is my responsibility as a mayor.

市民：1．しみん　　　2．いっみん　　3．いちみん　　4．いしみん

回答：1．かいとう　　2．まわごた　　3．まわこた　　4．かいと

市長：1．しちょう　　2．いちちょう　3．しちょ　　　4．いちちょ

c) 計算間違えたから、会社がつぶれてしまった！南極まで逃げようっと。

I made a calculation mistake and the company went under! I'm running away to Antarctica.

計算：1．はかさん　　2．はかざん　　3．けいさん　　4．けいざん

会社：1．しゃかい　　2．あいしゃ　　3．かいしゃ　　4．やしろ

南極：1．みなきょく　2．みなみきょく3．なんきょく　4．なきょく

3. Write the kanji (one or more) and the meaning of the following words.

きたぐち　　_____ _____　　なんべい　　_____ _____

やけん　　　_____ _____　　いちば　　　_____ _____

とうきょう　_____ _____　　しゃかい　　_____ _____

4. Correct either the reading or writing mistakes in the following words.

化海道	ほっかいどう	東洋	とうよう	大西洋	たいさいよう
東都	きょうと	抹茶	まちゃ	予山	よさん

Answers to exercises 練習解答

1. (Check them in the corresponding kanji tables #199, #202, #203, and #206)

2. a) 北西: 3 | 山里: 4 | 野菜: 3 // b) 市民: 1 | 回答: 1 | 市長: 1

c) 計算: 3 | 会社: 3 | 南極: 3

3. きたぐち: 北口, north exit | なんべい: 南米, South America | やけん: 野犬, stray dog

いちば: 市場, market | とうきょう: 東京, Tokyo | しゃかい: 社会, society

4. 北海道 ほっかいどう | 東洋 とうよう | 大西洋 たいせいよう

京都 きょうと | 抹茶 まっちゃ | 予算 よさん

Manga translation マンガ翻訳

Manager: Our company is known all over the world...

Manager (offscreen): We have branch offices throughout the country...

Manager (offscreen): From the smallest country village to the capital, Tokyo, we have shops in all cities...

Manager: And yet, the total amount of motor vehicles sold this year adds up to... zero!! Why?! We cannot leave this to take its own course!

Secretary: Tea. Our company markets tea, sir.

Manager: O-oh, of course... T-that is why...

New elements 新しい部首

未	even taller		毛 centipede	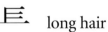
半	half		彡 long hair	
母	mother		心 broken heart	
兄	elder brother			

Lesson　19
第十九課

209 (3級)

YOUNGER SISTER

マイ
姉妹 (しまい) sisters
弟妹 (ていまい) younger brothers and sisters
姉妹都市 (しまいとし) sister cities

いもうと
妹 (いもうと) (my) younger sister
妹さん (いもうと) (someone else's) younger sister

く ㄅ 女 女
妇 妷 妹 妹

(8 strokes)

注 姉 (211)
姓 (Jōyō)
娘 (Jōyō)

学 A *younger sister* will always be like the tree that goes with her: a woman who must grow to be even taller.

特

210 (4級)

HALF, MIDDLE

ハン
前半戦 (ぜんはんせん) first half of a game
半島 (はんとう) peninsula
半生 (はんせい) half a lifetime
半値 (はんね) half price
半日 (はんにち) half day
大半 (たいはん) majority

なか(ば)
半ば (なか) half, middle

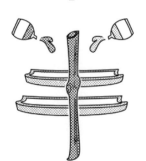

丶 丷 丷 ⺌
半

(5 strokes)

注 羊 (3rd)
平 (3rd)

学 Two slices of bread cut in *half* and seasoned with different sauces for people with different tastes. If they do not share, they will be whacked with a stick!

特 半 (alt)

ELDER SISTER

 く女女女′ 妒妒妼姉

(8 strokes)

姉姉 **姉** 姉
姉姉 **姉** **姉**

シ
姉妹 (しまい) sisters
姉妹語 (しまいご) sister languages
姉妹会社 (しまいがいしゃ)
affiliated companies

あね
姉 (あね) (my) elder sister
*お姉さん (ねえ)
elder sister, young woman

特 姉 (alt)

学 The *elder sister* is the woman in charge of going to the market.

注 妹 (209)
妊 (Jōyō)

FATHER

ノ ハ グ 父

(4 strokes)

トウ
お父さん (とう) father
父ちゃん (とう) dad, daddy

ちち
父 (ちち) dad
父親 (ちちおや) father

特 父 (alt)

学 Traditionally, the *father* is the one who earns the daily bread by the sweat of his brow.

注 交 (213)

213 (2級)

TO CROSS

、	二	六	六
亣	交		

(6 strokes)

コウ

外**交** diplomacy
がいこう

交渉 negotiations
こうしょう

交通 traffic
こうつう

交差点 intersection
こうさてん

交代 alternation, shift
こうたい

交番 police box
こうばん

ま(じる)

交じる to cross, to associate with, to mix with
まじる

注 父 (212)
校 (66)

学 You'll know him by his Mexican hat: he is the father, *crossing* the street to go to work.

特 交 (alt)

---

214 (4級)

MOTHER

L	ㄅ	口	母
母			

(5 strokes)

カ ア

お**母**さん mother, mom
かあ

ボ

母乳 mother's milk
ぼにゅう

母子 mother and child
ぼし

母性 maternity
ぼせい

母音 vowel
ぼいん

祖**母** grandmother
そぼ

はは

母 mother
はは

注 毎 (218)
海 (219)

学 This Japanese *mother* lovingly cradles her baby in her arms.

特

215 ELDER BROTHER (3級)

(5 strokes)

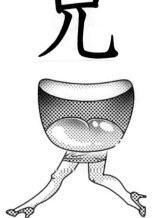

ケイ
兄事 to love someone as a brother
義兄 stepbrother

あに
兄 (my) elder brother
*お兄さん elder brother, young man (affectionate form of address)

 特

 学 My *elder brother*: a transvestite, big mouth.

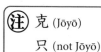 注 克 (Jōyō)
只 (not Jōyō)

216 HAIR (2級)

(4 strokes)

モウ
羊毛 wool
毛布 blanket
毛筆 writing / painting brush

け
毛 hair
髪の毛 hair (on the head)
眉毛 eyebrows
毛虫 caterpillar

 特

 学 Look at the silky *hair* of this nice centipede.

 注 手 (18)
羊 (3rd)

217 (4級) LONG, DIRECTOR

チョウ
店長 shop manager
てんちょう
校長 headmaster
こうちょう
会長 chairman
かいちょう
延長 extension
えんちょう
身長 one's height
しんちょう
成長 growth
せいちょう

なが(い)
長い long
なが

(8 strokes)

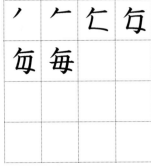

注 帳 (3rd)
張 (5th)

学 Look at the *long* hair of the maiden who waits a *long* time for her lover's letters.

特

218 (4級) EVERY

マイ
毎日 every day
まいにち
毎朝 every morning
まいあさ
毎晩 every night
まいばん
毎月 every month
まいつき
毎週 every week
まいしゅう
毎年 every year
まいとし
毎度 every time
まいど

(6 strokes)

注 母 (214)
海 (219)
毒 (4th)

学 Look at the mother in the shed. She is the person who will always be there for you, *every* day of your life.

特 毎 (alt)

219 (3級)

SEA

(9 strokes)

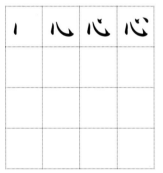

カイ
海中 open sea
海外 overseas
海岸 coast, beach
海軍 navy
黒海 Black Sea
地中海 Mediterranean

うみ
海 sea

特 海 (alt)

学 Look at the mother in the shed, next to the water. She is a sailor's mother, demanding the *sea* to give her back her son.

注 毎 (218)

---

220 (3級)

HEART, SOUL

心 心 心 心

(4 strokes)

シン
安心 peace of mind
心配 worry, anxiety
熱心 enthusiasm
心臓 the heart
心身 mind and body

こころ
心 heart, soul
心が優しい
　　　to be kind, tender

特

学 Pictogram of a broken *heart*.
Radical: 忄 or 心.

注 必 (4th)

こいつは明子(めいこ)。
ちょっとうるさいけど、
明(あか)るい妹だ。

毎年、夏休みに家族(かぞく)とともに
野村半島(のむらとう)へ行く。
海は楽しくて
大好(だいす)きだよ！

ぼく

ねーねー、兄ちゃん、遊(あそ)ぼう！

これ、お母さん。
長い髪(かみ)の毛をして
きれいなママだと思(おも)うのに、
叱(しか)ることが多いなぁ…
怒(おこ)ると怖(こわ)い！！

そして、お父さん。
普通(ふつう)に仕事(しごと)や
交通(こうつう)で機嫌(きげん)が
悪(わる)いけど、海に
着(つ)くと心が安(やす)らぐ
のだ！いつも若(わか)い
お姉ちゃんたちに
優(やさ)しい。

おかしいなぁ…
結局(けっきょく)、今年山奥(やまおく)に
キャンプすることに
した…なんでだろう？

Exercises 練習

1. Develop the stroke order of the following kanji.

母										
毛										
長										
心										

2. Choose the correct reading for each kanji or kanji combination.

a) 兄はバルセロナの姉妹都市である神戸で、店長をやっています。

My elder brother is a shop manager in Kobe, a sister city of Barcelona.

兄：　1．おに　　　　2．あに　　　　3．おにい　　　4．けい

姉妹：1．しいま　　　2．しまい　　　3．ましい　　　4．まいし

店長：1．てんちょう　2．てんちょ　　3．てんしょ　　4．みせなが

b) 日本と朝鮮半島の交渉は順調に進んでいますか？

Are the negotiations between Japan and the Korean peninsula progressing at a good pace?

半島：1．はんとう　　2．なかじま　　3．なかしま　　4．なじま

交渉：1．こしょ　　　2．こしょう　　3．こうしょ　　4．こうしょう

c) ダンサーになりたいので、毎日熱心に練習している。

I want to be a dancer, so I practice eagerly every day.

毎日：1．かいにち　　2．かいじつ　　3．まいにち　　4．まいじつ

熱心：1．ねごころ　　2．ねつごころ　3．ねつしん　　4．ねっしん

3. Write the kanji (one or more) and the meaning of the following words.

ちちおや　　＿＿＿＿　＿＿＿＿　　がいこう　　＿＿＿＿　＿＿＿＿

ぼいん　　　＿＿＿＿　＿＿＿＿　　けむし　　　＿＿＿＿　＿＿＿＿

まいとし　　＿＿＿＿　＿＿＿＿　　かいがい　　＿＿＿＿　＿＿＿＿

4. Correct either the reading or writing mistakes in the following words.

弟姉	ていまい	半値	ほんね	妹姉会社	しまいがいしゃ
母子	かあし	父通	こうつう	義兄	ぎあに
髪の毛	もののけ	地中毎	ちちゅうかい	火配	しんぱい

Answers to exercises 練習解答

1. (Check them in the corresponding kanji tables #214, #216, #217, and #220.)

2. a) 兄: 2 | 姉妹: 2 | 店長: 1 // b) 半島: 1 | 交渉: 4

   c) 毎日: 3 | 熱心: 4

3. ちちおや: 父親, father | がいこう: 外交, diplomacy | ぼいん: 母音, vowel

   けむし: 毛虫, caterpillar | まいとし: 毎年, every year | かいがい: 海外, overseas

4. 弟妹 ていまい | 半値 はんね | 姉妹会社 しまいがいしゃ | 母子 ぼし | 交通 こうつう

   義兄 ぎけい | 髪の毛 かみのけ | 地中海 ちちゅうかい | 心配 しんぱい

Manga translation マンガ翻訳

Text: Every year, during the summer holidays, I go with my family to the Nomura peninsula. I love the sea, it's great fun!

Inside the arrow: Me

Text: This is my younger sister, Meiko. She is a bit of pain, but she is very cheerful.

Younger sister: Come on, brother, come and play with me!

Text: This is mom. She is beautiful, with that long hair of hers, but she likes scolding too much... When she's angry, she's scary!

Text: And this is dad. He's usually in a bad mood, because of work or the traffic, but when he arrives at the beach, he relaxes: he's always very nice to young girls.

Text: That's weird... In the end, this year, we went camping far up in the mountains... I wonder why?

New elements 新しい部首

占	drinking water (compound)		馬	horse	
廿	hammock	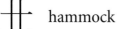	鳥	fire bird	

Lesson 20
第二十課

221 (3級)

TO THINK

思

シ
思想 thought
意志 will, intention
不思議 strange, mysterious

おも(う)
思う to think
思い出 a memory
思い直す to think better of

ー 口 冊 用
田 甲 思 思
思

(9 strokes)

思 思 **思** 思
思 思 **思** 思

注 界 (3rd)
　男 (74)

学 He who cultivates a rice field with all his heart, *thinks* on the well-being of all those he is going to feed.

特 恖 (alt)

222 (4級)

SHOP, STORE

店

テン
店員 clerk
書店 bookshop
喫茶店 coffee shop
百貨店 department store
飯店 Chinese restaurant

みせ
店 shop, store
酒店 liquor store

丶 亠 广 庁
庁 庐 店 店

(8 strokes)

店 店 **店** 店
店 店 店 **店**

注 点 (223)

学 The oldest *shop*, already in prehistoric times, is the drinking water shop. As you can see: inside a cave, there is a faucet to fill up mouths.

特 黙 (alt)

223

POINT

(2級)

(9 strokes)

点

テン

点 point
けってん
欠点 defect, flaw
まんてん
満点 perfect score, "10"
ちてん
地点 point, spot
てんじ
点字 Braille
ふってん
沸点 boiling point
てんか
点火 ignition, to kindle
ちょうてん
頂点 peak, zenith

特　学 In those times, a drinking water faucet and a good bonfire for warmth were enough to create a *point* for meeting.

注 店 (222)

224

REASON, LOGIC

(3級)

理

(11 strokes)

リ

りゆう
理由 reason
りろん
理論 theory
りょうり
料理 cooking, food
りょうりや
料理屋 restaurant
ふごうり
不合理 irrational, unreasonable
かんりにん
管理人 manager, supervisor
しゅうり
修理 repair

　 The king in the village is in charge of establishing *reason* among the inhabitants.

 里 (201)
黒 (226)
理 (Jōyō)

225 (2級)

YELLOW

き
黄 yellow
黄色い yellow (adj.)
黄身 egg yolk
黄水 bile

一	十	艹	共
芏	芑	带	黹
苗	黄	黄	

(11 strokes)

注 横 (3rd)
異 (6th)

学 Here you have a hammock that is going to be painted *yellow*: underneath, the legged-bucket bringing the paint.

特 黄 (alt)

212

226 (3級)

BLACK

コク
暗黒 darkness
黒板 blackboard
黒鉛 black lead, graphite
大黒柱 central pillar, mainstay

くろ(い)
黒い black
白黒 black and white
黒砂糖 brown sugar

丨	冂	日	日
甲	甲	里	里
黒	黒	黒	

(11 strokes)

注 里 (201)
理 (224)

学 Look how *black* everything is, after the village was enveloped in flames.

特 黒 (alt)

227

BRIGHTNESS, TO LIGHTEN

(3級)

```
｜ 冂 日 日
日 明 明 明
```
(8 strokes)

明 明 **明** 明
明 明 明 **明**

メイ

不明 ふめい unknown, unclear
自明 じめい obvious
説明 せつめい explanation
究明 きゅうめい investigation
発明 はつめい invention
照明 しょうめい lighting
明確 めいかく clear, well-defined

あか(るい)

明るい あか bright, light, cheerful

(特) 明 (alt)

(学) The sun and the moon are in charge of filling the world with *brightness*.

(注) 朋 (not Jōyō)
昭 (3rd)

213

228

FAIR, CLOUDLESS WEATHER

(2級)

```
｜ 冂 日 日
日 日 日 日
日 晴 晴 晴
```
(12 strokes)

晴 晴 **晴** 晴
晴 晴 晴 **晴**

セイ

晴天 せいてん clear weather
晴夜 せいや quiet night
晴朗 せいろう fair, clear

は(れる)

晴れ は fair weather
晴れる は to clear up
晴れ着 は ぎ one's best clothes

(特) 晴 (alt)
暒 (alt)

(学) Only when the weather is good and the sun shines in the *cloudless* sky do the blue plants grow on the moon.

(注) 青 (36)
清 (4th)
暗 (3rd)

229 (4級) FISH

ギョ
金魚 goldfish (きんぎょ)
人魚 mermaid (にんぎょ)
魚介 sea food (ぎょかい)
魚群 school of fish (ぎょぐん)
魚雷 torpedo (ぎょらい)

さかな
魚 fish (さかな)
魚屋 fish shop (さかなや)

(11 strokes)

注 漁 (4th)
黒 (226)

学 Camera flashes are striving to take photos of this rice field where, after being burned down by a fire, *fish* have been found. Radical: 魚 .

特 奐 (alt)

230 (2級) HORSE

バ
競馬 horse races (けいば)
競馬場 race track (けいばじょう)
馬力 horsepower (ばりき)
馬術 horseback riding (ばじゅつ)
白馬 white horse (はくば)
馬鹿 fool, idiot, stupid (ばか)

うま
馬 horse (うま)

(10 strokes)

注 駅 (3rd)
鳥 (231)

学 Pictogram of a *horse*.

特

(11 strokes)

BIRD

(3級)

231

チョウ
白鳥 swan
はくちょう
一石二鳥 "to kill two
いっせき に ちょう   birds with one stone"

とり
鳥 bird
とり
小鳥 small bird
ことり
渡り鳥 migratory bird
わた   どり
鳥居 torii, Shinto shrine
とりい   archway

特

学 Pictogram of the phoenix, a fire *bird*.

注 鳴 (232)
烏 (no Jōyō)
島 (3rd)

**TO SING, TO HOWL,
TO CRY, TO SOUND**

(2級)

232

メイ
悲鳴 moan, shriek
ひめい
雷鳴 thunder
らいめい
鳴動 rumbling
めいどう
共鳴 resonance
きょうめい

な（く）
鳴く to twitter, to caw,
な   to sing (animals)
鳴き声 cawing,
な   ごえ   bellowing, chirping,
howling, etc.

(14 strokes)

特

学 The fire bird *sings* with its mouth (beak).

注 鳥 (231)
烏 (not Jōyō)

毎晩、同じ夢を見るのです…

明るくて晴れた朝なのに、突然、暗くなります…

すると、「お腹がすいた」と思い、『北京飯店』へ行きます。歓迎をしてくれる方は黄色い馬です！

ひひひ、いらっしゃいませ！

ウエイターは黒い鳥で、カラスだと思います。魚のいいにおいがするんですが…

そのとたん、魚は自分だと気が付きます！ウエイターは喜んで鳴いています。

アホ
アホ

幸いに、沸騰点の前に、目が覚めます。不合理な夢でしょう…何の意味ですか？

まあ、まあ、安心してください。説明はとても簡単です…

それは、あなたの気が狂ったということですよ。

あ、そうか？すっきりした…ありがとう、先生！

Exercises 練習

1. Develop the stroke order of the following kanji.

店								
黄								
馬								
鳥								

2. Choose the correct reading for each kanji or kanji combination.

a) この<u>書店</u>の<u>欠点</u>はただ一つ：<u>店員</u>さんが本を読んだことのない人です！

This bookshop has only one flaw: the clerk hasn't read a single book in his whole life!

書店： 　1．しょうてん　2．しょてん　　3．かくみせ　　4．かきみせ

欠点： 　1．けってん　　2．けつでん　　3．けつてん　　4．けてん

店員： 　1．みせいん　　2．てにん　　　3．てんにん　　4．てんいん

b) <u>管理人</u>さんは<u>不思議</u>な人ですね… <u>魚介</u><ruby>料<rt>りょう</rt></ruby><ruby>理<rt>り</rt></ruby>だけしか食べないんだって。

The supervisor is a really strange person. They say she only eats seafood, just imagine.

管理人：1．かんしにん　2．かんりにん　3．かんじにん　4．かんにん

不思議：1．ふりぎ　　　2．ふしぎ　　　3．ふじぎ　　　4．ふおもぎ

魚介：1．さかなかい　2．さかかい　　3．ぎょうかい　4．ぎょかい

c) では、<u>黒板</u>を<ruby>使<rt>つか</rt></ruby>って、<ruby>問題<rt>もんだい</rt></ruby>を<u>明確</u>に<u>説明</u>してください。

Well, use the blackboard to explain the problem clearly.

黒板： 　1．くろばん　　2．ろくばん　　3．くこばん　　4．こくばん

明確： 　1．あかかく　　2．あっかく　　3．あかがく　　4．めいかく

説明： 　1．せつあか　　2．せつべい　　3．せつねい　　4．せつめい

3. Write the kanji (one or more) and the meaning of the following words.

おもいで　　 _____ _____　　きいろい　　 _____ _____

しろくろ　　 _____ _____　　にんぎょ　　 _____ _____

いっせきにちょう _____ _____　　なきごえ　　 _____ _____

4. Correct either the reading or writing mistakes in the following words.

料理	りりょう	鳥鹿	ばか	喫茶点	きっさてん
寅水	きみず	里砂糖	くろざとう	青れる	はれる

Answers to exercises 練習解答

1. (Check them in the corresponding kanji tables #222, #225, #230, and #231)

2. a) 書店:2 | 欠点:1 | 店員:4 // b) 管理人:2 | 不思議:2 | 魚介:4 // c) 黒板:4 | 明確:4 | 説明:4

3. おもいで: 思い出, a memory | きいろい: 黄色い, yellow-colored

しろくろ: 白黒, black and white | にんぎょ: 人魚, mermaid | いっせきにちょう: 一石二鳥, "to kill two birds with one stone" | なきごえ: 泣き声, cawing, bellowing, chirping, etc.

4. 料理 りょうり | 馬鹿 ばか | 喫茶店 きっさてん

黄水 きみず | 黒砂糖 くろざとう | 晴れる はれる

Manga translation マンガ翻訳

Patient: Every night I have the same dream...

Patient (offscreen): It's a bright and clear morning, but it suddenly becomes dark...

Patient (offscreen): Then I realize I'm hungry, and I go the "Beijing Chinese restaurant." At the door I'm greeted by a yellow horse!

Chinese horse: Weeeiiiihhelcome!

Patient (offscreen): The waiter is a black bird, a crow, I think. There's a delicious smell of fish, but...

Patient (offscreen): ...Just then, I realize I'm the fish! The waiter caws merrily.

Crow: caw, caw

Patient: Fortunately, just before reaching the boiling point, I wake up... It's a very illogical dream, isn't it? What can it mean?

Doctor: Nothing, nothing, don't worry. It has a very simple explanation...

Doctor: ...it's just that you've gone crazy.

Patient: Oh, really? Well, that's a relief... Thank you, doctor!

New elements 新しい部首

矢 gigantic arrow

弓 bow

氵 ice cubes

丷 horns

Lesson 21
第二十一課

233 (1級)

ARROW

矢

や

- 矢 (や) arrow
- 矢先 (やさき) arrowhead, target
- 毒矢 (どくや) poisoned arrow
- 矢文 (やぶみ) letter tied to an arrow
- 火矢 (ひや) flaming arrow

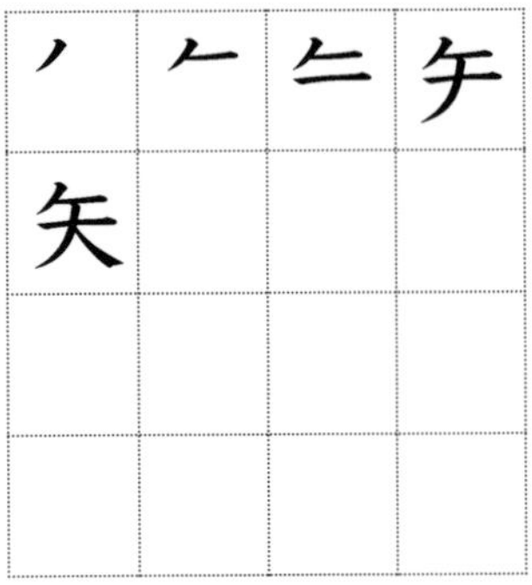

(5 strokes)

矢	矢	矢	矢
矢	矢	矢	矢

注 失 (4th)
禾 (not Jōyō)
天 (68)

学 Here is the representation of a gigantic *arrow* (or an *arrow*-giant), who is boring a hole in the shed where it's been shut in. Radical: 矢 .

特 笶 (alt)

234 (3級)

TO KNOW, TO LEARN

知

チ

- 無知 (むち) ignorance
- 知名 (ちめい) famous
- 知恵 (ちえ) wisdom, intelligence
- 知覚 (ちかく) perception
- 知識人 (ちしきじん) intellectual

し(る)

- 知る (しる) to know, to learn
- 知り合い (しりあい) acquaintance

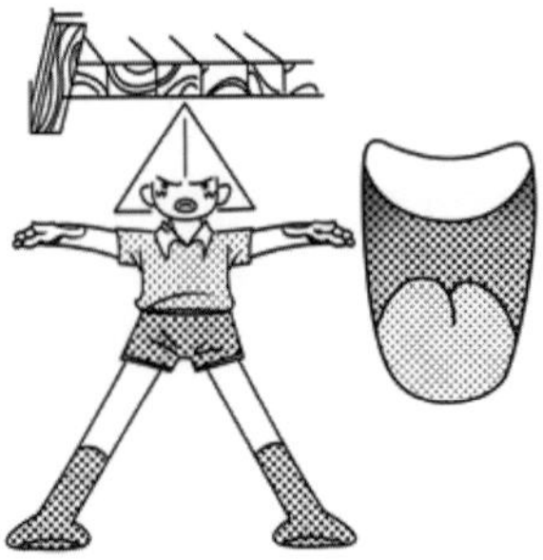

(8 strokes)

知	知	知	知
知	知	知	知

注 和 (3rd)
味 (3rd)

学 Only the person who *knows* how to do it, can throw gigantic arrows through the mouth.

特

235 — BOW (1級)

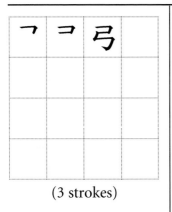

ㄱ　コ　弓

(3 strokes)

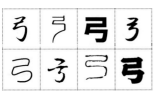

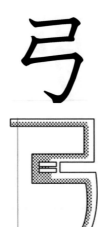

キュウ
弓道（きゅうどう） traditional Japanese archery

ゆみ
弓（ゆみ） bow
弓矢（ゆみや） bow and arrows
弓を引く（ゆみをひく） to draw a bow
弓弦（ゆみづる） bowstring
石弓（いしゆみ） crossbow, catapult

 特

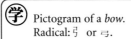 学 Pictogram of a *bow*.
Radical: 弓 or ⼸.

注 引 (236)
　己 (6th)

---

236 — TO PULL, TO WITHDRAW (3級)

ㄱ　コ　弓　引

(4 strokes)

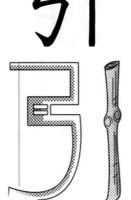

イン
引力（いんりょく） gravitation
引退（いんたい） to retire

ひ(く)
引く（ひ） to pull, to withdraw
値引き（ねびき） discount
割引き（わりびき） discount
引き出し（ひきだし） drawer
引っ越し（ひっこし） house-moving

 特

 学 Use the bow to *pull* and fire an arrow at the stick.

 注 弓 (235)
　弱 (237)
　弔 (Jōyō)

221

237 (3級)

WEAK, FEEBLE

ジャク
弱点 weak point
病弱 delicate constitution
薄弱 feeble, flimsy

よわ(い)
弱い weak
弱気 shyness
弱虫 coward
弱火 low heat

ヿ コ 弓 弓
弓 引 引 弱
弱 弱

(10 strokes)

弱 弱 **弱** 弱
弱 弱 弱 **弱**

注 引 (236)
羽 (140)

学 Two *weak* bows because they've frozen and anything will splinter them. (Be careful with the new component of "ice," derived from water.)

特 弱 (alt)

238 (3級)

STRONG

キョウ
強力 power, strength
強国 great power,
        strong country
強調 emphasis

ゴウ
強奪 extortion, violence
強情 stubbornness

つよ(い)
強い strong

ヿ コ 弓 弘
弘 弘 弘 弘
弾 強 強

(11 strokes)

強 強 **強** 強
強 強 強 **強**

注 兎 (not Jōyō)
弦 (Jōyō)

学 The image of a *strong* bug: armed with a bow, and with unlimited provisions, thanks to the cornucopia.

特 強 (alt)

239 — YOUNGER BROTHER （3級）

(7 strokes)

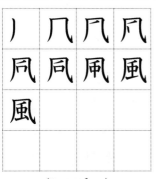

テイ
師弟 (してい) teacher and pupil
弟子 (でし) pupil, disciple
孝弟 (こうてい) respect towards parents and elder brothers and sisters
徒弟 (とてい) apprentice
末弟 (まってい) the youngest brother

おとうと
弟 (おとうと) younger brother

特

学 My *younger brother*: a horned archer who is frustrated because his arrow has broken.

注 弗 (not Jōyō)
第 (3rd)
弔 (Jōyō)

240 — WIND, BREEZE, STYLE （3級）

(9 strokes)

フウ
台風 (たいふう) typhoon
作風 (さくふう) literary style
強風 (きょうふう) gale
風船 (ふうせん) balloon
和風 (わふう) Japanese style

かぜ
風 (かぜ) wind
神風 (かみかぜ) divine wind

特 凡 (simp)
凨 (alt)

学 The bug cries under its new wig... Because the *wind* is blowing it away! (Be careful with the effect of the wind on the wig's right end.)

注 周 (4th)

Exercises 練習

1. Develop the stroke order of the following kanji.

弓							
弱							
弟							
風							

2. Choose the correct reading for each kanji or kanji combination.

a) <u>弱い</u> <u>弟子</u>はいやだ。<ruby>君<rt>きみ</rt></ruby>が<u>弱虫</u>ならささっと帰りたまえ。

   I don't like weak disciples. If you're a coward, you can leave straight away.

   弱い：　　1．つよい　　　2．づよい　　　3．よわい　　　4．ようわい

   弟子：　　1．ていし　　　2．でし　　　　3．でじ　　　　4．ていこ

   弱虫：　　1．じゃくちゅう　2．よわむし　　3．しゃくちゅう　4．ようわむし

b) <u>弓道</u>をやっている<u>知り合い</u>はいないの？

   Don't you have any acquaintances who practice traditional Japanese archery?

   弓道：　　1．きゅどう　　2．きゅうどう　　3．ゆみち　　　4．ゆみみち

   知り合い：1．ちりあい　　2．ちりごいい　　3．しりあい　　4．しりごい

c) 今回のスピーチでは「<u>知恵</u>を<ruby>尊敬<rt>そんけい</rt></ruby>すべきだ」と<u>強調</u>していた。

   This time, the speech has emphasized that "wisdom must be respected."

   知恵：　　1．しえ　　　　2．じえ　　　　3．ちえ　　　　4．ぢえ

   強調：　　1．つよちょう　2．ごうちょう　3．きょちょう　4．きょうちょう

3. Write the kanji (one or more) and the meaning of the following words.

やさき	_____ _____	ちめい	_____ _____
ひきだし	_____ _____	じゃくてん	_____ _____
きょうこく	_____ _____	たいふう	_____ _____

4. Correct either the reading or writing mistakes in the following words.

知識人	ちしきにん	毒天	どくや	右弓	いしゆみ
弓カ	いんりょく	強情	きょうじょう	弟	おとと
和風	わがせ	割引き	わりひき	強よい	つよい

Answers to exercises 練習解答

1. (Check them in the corresponding kanji tables #235, #237, #239, and #240.)

2. a) 弱い: 3 | 弟子: 2 | 弱虫: 2 // b) 弓道: 2 | 知り合い: 3 // c) 知恵: 3 | 強調: 4

3. やさき: 矢先, arrowhead, target | ちめい: 知名, famous

ひきだし: 引き出し, drawer | じゃくてん: 弱点, weak point

きょうこく: 強国, great power, strong country | たいふう: 台風, typhoon

4. 知識人 | ちしきじん | 毒矢 どくや | 石弓 いしゆみ | 引力 いんりょく

強情 ごうじょう | 弟 おとうと | 和風 わふう | 割引き わりびき | 強まい つよい

Manga translation マンガ翻訳

Voices (offscreen): Wow! Very good!

Sound of the arrow striking: Thack

Archer: Ha, ha, ha, ha! I'm the strongest! So, isn't there anybody who can do it better than me?

Voice (offscreen): Yes, me!

Archer: Hmm? Who are you?

Bobin: I'm Bobin Hood!

Text panel: (Robin's younger brother)

Archer: Where has this flimsy pipsqueak come out from? He probably doesn't even have the strength to draw the bow!

Background laughter: Ha, ha, ha Ho, ho, ho

Archer: I knew it, he doesn't have a clue about shooting!

Background laughter: Ha, ha, ha

Sound of the inhaling and exhaling: Haaah, fooooh!

Sound of the arrow striking: Thak

Archer: ...

Voice (offscreen): In...in only one blow...

Archer: He... he beat me...

Supporters: Hooray! Long live "Bobin the Strong Winded!"

Review of Grade 2

小学校二年生
まとめ問題

Review Grade 2　二年生・まとめ問題

1. Link the kanji with their corresponding *kun'yomi* and *on'yomi* readings.

1.	あたま	歩	ライ
2.	ある(く)	方	ホウ
3.	いま	船	ホ
4.	う(る)	今	バイ
5.	か(く)	書	トウ
6.	かお	売	セン
7.	かた	光	ショ
8.	く(る)	来	サク
9.	くも	作	コン
10.	つく(る)	雲	コウ
11.	ひか(る)	頭	ガン
12.	ふね	顔	ウン

2. Write the kanji missing in the following text.

お＿＿さんが＿＿＿＿に＿＿ったことがあったなんて＿＿りませんでした。僕が
＿＿っているかぎり、＿＿＿＿＿で＿＿員をしていた、＿＿葉も＿＿達も＿＿な
い＿＿です。＿＿＿＿に＿＿うと、＿＿が好きなのか、＿＿が嫌いなのか、＿＿でも
＿＿かりません。＿＿いたことありません。僕らの＿＿＿＿は「ただいま」、「あ、お＿＿
り」だけです。よく＿＿えてみると、普＿＿に＿＿したことは＿＿＿＿もないです。

I didn't know my father had gone overseas. As far as I know, he is a man of few words, few friends, and a clerk in a secondhand book store. Frankly, not even now do I know what he likes or dislikes. I have never asked him. Our conversations are only: "I'm home," and "oh, okay." Now that I think of it, not once have we ever talked normally.

しかし、この＿＿＿、＿＿き＿＿しの＿＿にあった、お＿＿さんが＿＿＿＿＿
さい＿＿＿＿＿に＿＿いた＿＿を＿みました。そこには、＿＿＿が＿＿＿＿で
暮らしていた頃の経験を＿＿っています。＿＿＿＿驚いたのはニューヨークで＿＿り
＿＿った＿＿＿＿の＿＿＿の＿＿＿の＿＿です。それは、お＿＿さんよ
り＿＿の＿＿、彼の初恋の人でした。

But, the other day, I read a diary that was in a drawer, and that my father had written when he was 25. There, he narrated his experiences from the time he lived in the U.S. What surprised me most was the story of the calligraphy teacher, a Japanese woman he met in New York. She was his first love, the woman before my mother.

3. Choose the correct reading for each kanji or kanji combination.

a) <u>店長</u>はすぐ<u>心配</u>する人だから、<u>毎日</u>必ず<u>顔</u>を出します。

The shop manager worries right away, so he comes every day to put in an appearance.

店長:　　1．みせなが　　2．みせな　　3．てんちょ　　4．てんちょう

心配:　　1．こころはい　　2．ここはい　　3．しんはい　　4．しんぱい

毎日:　　1．まいにち　　2．かいにち　　3．うみび　　4．うみひ

顔:　　　1．あたま　　2．がん　　3．かお　　4．とう

b) <u>髪の毛</u>の長いお<u>姉</u>ちゃんは人気者。昔の<u>祖母</u>と<u>同じ</u>だ。

My elder sister, the long-haired one, is a heartbreaker. She's like my grandmother long ago.

髪の毛:　1．かみのもう　2．かみのも　3．かみのけ　4．かみのげ

姉:　　　1．あね　　2．に　　3．まい　　4．ねえ

祖母:　　1．そぼう　　2．そぼ　　3．そはは　　4．そかあ

同じ:　　1．どうじ　　2．とうじ　　3．おなじ　　4．なおじ

c) 車で行きたいの！？なんて<u>無茶</u>な！この<u>交通</u>状態じゃ、<u>間に合</u>わないよ！

Do you want to go by car?! That's crazy! With this traffic, we'll never make it in time!

無茶:　　1．むさ　　2．むちゃ　　3．むだ　　4．むちゃあ

交通:　　1．こつ　　2．こうつ　　3．こつう　　4．こうつう

間に合:　1．かにあ　　2．げにあ　　3．かんにあ　　4．まにあ

4. Choose the correct kanji for each reading.

a) <u>かぜ</u>の<u>たに</u>のナウシカというジブリの<u>えいが</u>を<u>し</u>らない？

Don't you know Ghibli's film, Nausicaä of the Valley of the Wind?

かぜ:　　　1．虫　　2．更　　3．風　　4．夙

たに:　　　1．谷　　2．合　　3．容　　4．公

えいが:　　1．映面　　2．映画　　3．映田　　4．映由

し(らない):　1．朱　　2．天　　3．矢　　4．知

b) <u>ちず</u>があっても、<u>がいこく</u>の<u>みち</u>は分からないよ！

I may have a map, but I don't understand foreign streets!

ちず:　　　1．池図　　2．池区　　3．地図　　4．地区

がいこく:　1．外園　　2．名園　　3．外国　　4．名国

みち:　　　1．道　　2．首　　3．百　　4．近

c) <u>しんぶん</u>に出たよ！そう、<u>きんじょ</u>の<u>さかなや</u>よ。

It's in the newspaper! Yes, our neighborhood's fish shop.

しんぶん:　1．新問　　2．親問　　3．新聞　　4．親聞

きんじょ:　1．斤所　　2．近所　　3．返所　　4．金所

さかなや:　1．魚室　　2．魚屋　　3．黒室　　4．黒屋

Answers to exercises 練習解答

1.

ある(く)	歩	ホ
かた	方	ホウ
ふね	船	セン
いま	今	コン
か(く)	書	ショ
う(る)	売	バイ
ひか(る)	光	コウ
く(る)	来	ライ
つく(る)	作	サク
くも	雲	ウン
あたま	頭	トウ
かお	顔	ガン

2.　お父さんが海外に行ったことがあったなんて知りませんでした。僕（ぼく）が知っているかぎり、古本屋で店員をしていた、言葉も友達（だち）も少ない人です。正直に言うと、何が好きなのか、何が嫌（きら）いなのか、今でも分かりません。聞いたことありません。僕（ぼく）らの会話は「ただいま」、「あ、お帰（ふ）り」だけです。よく考えてみると、普通に話したことは一回もないです。

　　しかし、この間、引き出しの中にあった、お父さんが二十五才の時に書いた日記を読みました。そこには、自分が米国で暮（く）らしていた頃（ころ）の経験（けいけん）を語っています。一番驚（おどろ）いたのはニューヨークで知り合った日本人の書道の先生の話です。それは、お母さんより前の女、彼（かれ）の初恋（はつこい）の人でした。

3. a) 店長: 4 | 心配: 4 | 毎日: 1 | 顔: 3

　　b) 髪の毛: 3 | お姉ちゃん: 4 | 祖母: 2 | 同じ: 3

　　c) 無茶: 2 | 交通: 4 | 間に合う: 4

4. a) かぜ: 3 | たに: 1 | えいが: 2 | し(らない): 4

　　b) ちず: 3 | がいこく: 3 | みち: 1

　　c) しんぶん: 3 | きんじょ: 2 | さかなや: 2

Indexes
索引

233

Readings index 読み方索引

H

HA	ハ	羽	140
HACHI	ハチ	八	9
ha(eru/yasu)	は(える/やす)	生	35
haha	はは	母	214
hai(ru)	はい(る)	入	58
haka(ru)	はか(る)	計	106
haka(ru)	はか(る)	図	183
HAKU	ハク	白	37
HAN	ハン	半	210
hana	はな	花	70
hana(su)	はな(す)	話	107
hane	はね	羽	140
hara	はら	原	120
ha(reru)	は(れる)	晴	228
haru	はる	春	156
hashi(ru)	はし(る)	走	191
haya(i/meru/maru)	はや(い/める/まる)	早	39
hayashi	はやし	林	62
hazu(su)	はず(す)	外	128
hi	ひ	日	33
hi	ひ	火	54
hidari	ひだり	左	30
higashi	ひがし	東	199
hikari	ひかり	光	115
hika(ru)	ひか(る)	光	115
hi(ku)	ひ(く)	引	236
hiro(i/garu/meru)	ひろ(い/がる/める)	広	98
hiru	ひる	昼	143
hito	ひと	一	1
hito	ひと	人	57
HO	ホ	歩	88
HŌ	ホウ	方	90
HOKU	ホク	北	197
HON	ホン	本	60
hoshi	ほし	星	147
hoso(i)	ほそ(い)	細	122
HYAKU	ヒャク	百	38

I

ichi	いち	市	203
ICHI	イチ	一	1
ie	いえ	家	125
ike	いけ	池	168
i(kiru/kasu)	い(きる/かす)	生	35
i(kiru)	い(きる)	活	166
i(ku)	い(く)	行	136
ima	いま	今	102
imōto	いもうと	妹	209
IN	イン	音	43
IN	イン	引	236
inu	いぬ	犬	48
iro	いろ	色	188
i(ru/reru)	い(る/れる)	入	58
ishi	いし	石	12
ito	いと	糸	50
itsu(tsu)	いつ(つ)	五	6
i(u)	い(う)	言	105
iwa	いわ	岩	160

J

JAKU	ジャク	弱	237
JI	ジ	耳	21
JI	ジ	字	77
JI	ジ	寺	123
JI	ジ	時	124
JI	ジ	地	169
JI	ジ	自	173
JIKI	ジキ	直	104
JIN	ジン	人	57
JITSU	ジツ	日	33
JO	ジョ	女	75
JŌ	ジョウ	上	2
JŌ	ジョウ	場	170
JŪ	ジュウ	十	27

K

ka	か	日	33
KA	カ	下	3
KA	カ	火	54
KA	カ	花	70
KA	カ	家	125
KA	カ	夏	149
KA	カ	科	153
KA	カ	歌	196
KAA	カア	母	214
kado	かど	門	132
kado	かど	角	187
kae(ru)	かえ(る)	帰	163
KAI	カイ	貝	23
KAI	カイ	会	100
KAI	カイ	絵	117
KAI	カイ	回	159
KAI	カイ	海	219
ka(ku)	か(く)	書	113
KAKU	カク	画	184
KAKU	カク	角	187
kami	かみ	紙	118
KAN	カン	間	133
kane	かね	金	17
kanga(eru)	かんが(える)	考	83
kao	かお	顔	172
kara	から	空	67
karada	からだ	体	190
kata	かた	方	90
katachi	かたち	形	189
katana	かたな	刀	91
kata(ru)	かた(る)	語	108
KATSU	カツ	活	166
ka(u)	か(う)	買	111
kawa	かわ	川	51
kayo(u)	かよ(う)	通	186
kaze	かぜ	風	240
kazo(eru)	かぞ(える)	数	82
kazu	かず	数	82
ke	け	毛	216
KE	ケ	気	52
KE	ケ	家	125
KEI	ケイ	計	106
KEI	ケイ	形	189

KEI	ケイ	兄	215	KYŪ	キュウ	休	61
KEN	ケン	見	24	KYŪ	キュウ	弓	235
KEN	ケン	犬	48	**M**			
ki	き	木	59	ma	ま	間	133
ki	き	黄	225	machi	まち	町	73
KI	キ	気	52	mae	まえ	前	158
KI	キ	記	109	MAI	マイ	妹	209
KI	キ	帰	163	MAI	マイ	毎	218
KI	キ	汽	167	ma(jiru)	ま(じる)	交	213
ki(ku/koeru)	き(く/こえる)	聞	134	MAN	マン	万	89
KIN	キン	金	17	mana(bu)	まな(ぶ)	学	78
KIN	キン	近	178	maru(i)	まる(い)	円	20
kita	きた	北	197	maru(i)	まる(い)	丸	92
ki(ru)	き(る)	切	94	mawa(ru/su)	まわ(る/す)	回	159
ko	こ	小	49	me	め	目	22
ko	こ	木	59	me	め	女	75
ko	こ	子	76	MEI	メイ	名	46
KO	コ	古	103	MEI	メイ	明	227
KO	コ	戸	131	MEI	メイ	鳴	232
KŌ	コウ	口	10	michi	みち	道	175
KŌ	コウ	校	65	migi	みぎ	右	29
KŌ	コウ	考	83	mimi	みみ	耳	21
KŌ	コウ	公	97	minami	みなみ	南	198
KŌ	コウ	広	98	mi(ru/eru/seru)	み(る/える/せる)	見	24
KŌ	コウ	光	115	mise	みせ	店	222
KŌ	コウ	行	136	mi(ttsu)	み(っつ)	三	5
KŌ	コウ	工	138	mizu	みず	水	53
KŌ	コウ	後	157	MŌ	モウ	毛	216
KŌ	コウ	高	193	mochi(iru)	もち(いる)	用	185
KŌ	コウ	交	213	MOKU	モク	目	22
koe	こえ	声	112	MOKU	モク	木	59
kokono	ここの	九	25	MON	モン	文	66
kokoro	こころ	心	220	MON	モン	門	132
KOKU	コク	石	12	mori	もり	森	63
KOKU	コク	谷	95	moto	もと	本	60
KOKU	コク	国	182	moto	もと	元	116
KOKU	コク	黒	226	mugi	むぎ	麦	150
koma(kai)	こま(かい)	細	122	mui	むい	六	7
kome	こめ	米	81	mura	むら	村	64
KON	コン	今	102	muro	むろ	室	126
kota(eru)	こた(える)	答	208	mushi	むし	虫	14
koto	こと	言	105	mu(ttsu)	む(っつ)	六	7
KU	ク	九	25	MYŌ	ミョウ	名	46
KU	ク	工	138	**N**			
KŪ	クウ	空	67	na	な	名	46
kubi	くび	首	174	naga(i)	なが(い)	長	217
kuchi	くち	口	10	NAI	ナイ	内	127
kuda(ru)	くだ(る)	下	3	naka	なか	中	13
kumi	くみ	組	121	naka(ba)	なか(ば)	半	210
kumo	くも	雲	164	na(ku)	な(く)	鳴	232
kuni	くに	国	182	nama	なま	生	35
kuro(i)	くろ(い)	黒	226	nan	なん	何	195
ku(ru)	く(る)	来	135	NAN	ナン	男	74
kuruma	くるま	車	32	NAN	ナン	南	198
kusa	くさ	草	69	nana(tsu)	なな(つ)	七	8
ku(u)	く(う)	食	130	nani	なに	何	195
KYŌ	キョウ	教	84	nao(su)	なお(す)	直	104
KYŌ	キョウ	京	204	natsu	なつ	夏	149
KYŌ	キョウ	強	238	ne	ね	音	43
KYŪ	キュウ	九	25				